MEN, MACHINES & MAINTENANCE at Exmouth Junction

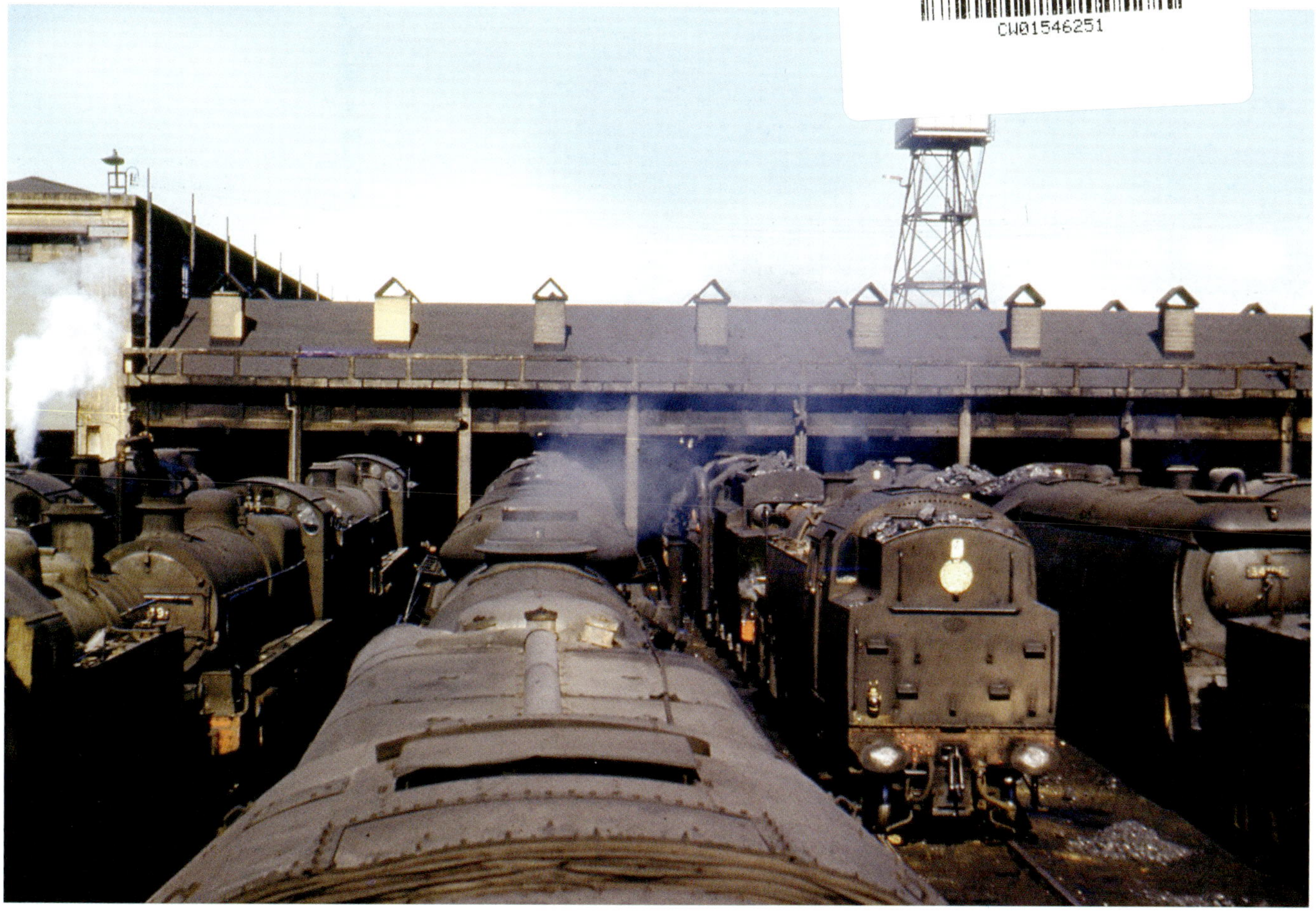

- a personal perspective

Robert E Trevelyan

© Noodle Books and Robert E Trevelyan 2013 ISBN 978-1-906419-84-4

First published in 2013 by Kevin Robertson under the **NOODLE BOOKS** imprint
PO Box 279 Corhampton, SOUTHAMPTON SO32 3ZX

The Publisher and Author hereby give notice that all rights to this work are reserved. Aside from brief passages for the purpose of review, no part of this work may be reproduced, copied by electronic or other means, or otherwise stored in any information storage and retrieval system without written permission from the Publisher. This includes the illustrations herein which shall remain the copyright of the copyright holder unless otherwise stated.

www.noodlebooks.co.uk

Printed in England by Berforts Information Press Ltd.
.

Publishers note: Every effort has been made to identify and correctly annotate photographic credits. Should an error have occurred then this is entirely unintentional.

Preface

True Railwaymen are members of a large and close family and these family ties continue long after their time at work is over, their friendships lasting until the grave.

The care shown to one another is evident when one visits the annual retirement gathering in April at The Corn Exchange in Exeter. This has now been organised on a volunteer basis for 50 years and, with most of the men now in their seventies and eighties, it never ceases to amaze me the care each has for the others. Equally gratifying is to witness the same care in the younger generation with the way they organise the event. Other activities include the 'Green Badge' gathering every November at the Exmouth Junction Railway Club.

I first came across this care when I started at Exmouth Junction as a 16-year-old apprentice fitter. I had been at Swindon for a year, on a first year course, and now I was where I had always wanted to be, on the railway and part of the family. Working on the railway is a vocation every bit as much as that of a farmer, doctor, teacher or carer, it courses through your veins and works so deeply into your heart that you want to eat it, drink it - and sometimes spit it out! Such is the effect that it never leaves and becomes a part of who you are, this being true for every grade, be the individual a cleaner or top manager. Of course not everyone who worked, or works, on the railway feels the same but for those who have the infection, there is no cure, no matter how long you may later be away from it.

This book is therefore dedicated not only to the men and women who worked at Exmouth Junction Motive Power Depot (MPD), but to all those who feel themselves members of the 'family', nationwide.

Bob Trevelyan
Newton Abbot   February 2013

Front cover, top - *Driver Cordier oiling T9 No.30718 at Okehampton on 19th August 1960.*

Front cover, centre - *Drummond M7 No.30667 outside the shed on 7th April 1963. The caption and photo for this appears on Page 5.*

Front cover, bottom - *No.35008 'Orient Line' inside the 'Cathedral' with its wheels removed. The caption and photo for this appears on Page 52.*
W Philip Connolly/Robert Humm collection

Rear cover, top - *W class No.31912 pilots No.4996 on the Westbury to Exeter Central cement, banked by Nos.31924-16 on 2nd March. Alongside is No.34002 on the 2.20pm Ilfracombe to Waterloo.*

Rear cover, bottom - *The 13.25 to Salisbury East Yard leaves Exmouth Junction Goods Yard behind class No.34078 '222 Squadron' on 29th June 1964, with 72A (by now 83D) glimpsed in the background.*

Frontispiece - *Busy days at Exmouth Junction, probably a Sunday, bearing in mind the number of engines seen. The scene was recorded from a privileged vantage point!*
Photo: Amyas Crump collection

Opposite page - *Salisbury shed's No.30453 'King Arthur' is seen outside the depot between duties.*
Photo: Amyas Crump collection

Left - *The Author aged 16 with 'Ginger' Discombe, 22nd October 1965.*
Photo: E Crawforth

Contents

	Introduction	5
1	Exmouth Junction - A Personal History	7
2.	A Short History of Exmouth Junction shed	13
3.	Men of The Junction	29
4.	The Breakdown Gang and First Aid Group	57
5.	Exmouth Engines and Working The Shed	63
6.	The Meldon Ballast	79
7.	The End - Rundown and Closure	87
	Appendices	93

No.82024, a BR Standard class 3 2-6-2 tank, 10 of which were allocated to Exmouth Junction from new to work the busy Exmouth branch commuter services along with a series of BR 63' suburban carriages, is seen about to diverge onto the Exmouth branch. These locomotives also worked the Sidmouth Branch from both Exmouth and Sidmouth Junction as well as the Bude line. Freight stock on the level sidings of the Exmouth Jct Goods Yard emphasises the steep gradient up from Exeter Central station on the main line, which levels out at the junction itself.
Photo: E Crawforth.

Introduction

It is now over 45 years since the last steam locomotive in revenue service on British Railways had its fire dropped and a 150 year old era came to an end. On that day in August 1968 it wasn't only the end of the steam locomotive, but the end of a way of life, together with the infrastructure that supported it.

By comparison with the plethora of books produced on engines themselves, few have been written about the locomotive sheds, or depots, and particularly the men who worked in them, men who played a vital part, being involved in the running, servicing and maintenance of the steam locomotives based there.

Of those who have put pen to paper, only one has really sought to describe the effectual working of the sheds and the difference between the railways and the regions. R N N Hardy, in his excellent book *Steam in the Blood*, goes a long way, but tends to keep to the footplate side, understandable in that the book is written in an autobiographical style. E S Beavor has written possibly the most comprehensive series of books on the subject. *Steam Was My Calling* is an autobiography, whilst *Steam Motive Power Depots* is a critique, covering as it does the complete working of the steam locomotive shed.

In *Steam Was My Calling* I came across this phrase: *"There is also a wealth of folklore associated with steam power, and with other superseded aspects of railway working, which is destined to be lost to posterity unless we, whose lives were bound up with those functions, are prepared to record it".*

Reading these words, I determined to record the experiences of working in the steam sheds by those who worked there. It is always better, we are told, to write about something you know, so this is about one shed in particular, Exmouth Junction Motive Power Depot (as it became known after nationalisation), the men, and the work that was carried out there. It is more than just about the footplate staff - for much has already been written about that particular aspect - it is about all the staff, from the District Motive Power Superintendent to the Shed Labourer. The intention of what follows is to show how they all intertwined, achieving the best results always being paramount in their minds. The fact that this was actually achieved is a credit to them all and was because they knew the importance of working together.

Dugald Drummond's class M7 0-4-4 tanks were associated with Exmouth Junction until their last years in the early 1960s. They served many functions, No.30667 seen here being an example of the pull-push fitted members of the class which worked on the East Devon branch lines such as that to Seaton and the lines to Exmouth itself, the Standard class 3s never completely eclipsing them. They were also used on local goods duties and as station pilots at Exeter Central.

30667 was an interesting machine. The original engine of this number was a short-framer but what is seen here was actually 30106, renumbered for accountancy reasons! Mike Daly is seen at the rear of the engine and 31818 is in the shed, on 7th April 1963.
Photo: Maurice Dart.

Exmouth Junction was the principal locomotive shed for the Southern Region (and its predecessors') lines in the West of England. All trains to the 'Withered Arm' lines beyond Exeter had to travel over Western Region lines at Exeter St Davids, the line from there up to Exeter Central rising on a 1 in 37 gradient.

This meant that Exmouth Junction had to supply banking engines for heavy trains from the west, notably the Meldon ballast trains, workings of which are related later in this book. There was also a cement works at Exeter Central as well as the concrete works at Exmouth Junction, trains to which came in over Western metals from Westbury. All kinds of Southern tank engines were sent west to work these and here we see two of the Maunsell class W 2-6-4 tanks (Nos.31914/24) giving a helping hand to an unidentified Western 'Hall' and Standard class 4 tank No.80035 at Exeter St Davids in 1963.   *Both: Amyas Crump collection*

Chapter 1
Exmouth Junction - a personal history

If you have ever stood in a Cathedral or in an empty football stadium and been overawed by its enormity and presence, then you might, just might, get an inkling of what I felt when I walked up the path past the sign that said

'BRITISH RAILWAYS, SOUTHERN REGION, EXMOUTH JUNCTION MOTIVE POWER DEPOT. STRICTLY NO ADMITTANCE UNLESS AUTHORISED'.

It was with a slightly superior feeling knowing that I had that authority that I went beyond the sign and on into that hallowed place that held such secrets and mysteries.

On a grey autumn day in 1960 this was a school Railway Club outing organised by our leader, the geography master G D Massey, and I was a new member on my first shed visit. We were told to wait at the entrance whilst he presented our pass to the man in charge. While we waited we could glimpse something of what was to come, steam engines - and lots of them. Mr Massey returned with a guide and the tour began, we passed between the 12 roads, row upon row of engines, some in steam and quietly simmering, others cold awaiting attention of some sort. We were busy writing down numbers, "Oh look a T9" said one, another exclaimed "An Adams Radial" and so on. Being so close beside the engines, the size of them was too much for me to take in. I just gazed in

This view of Exmouth Junction was taken from alongside the disposal roads on 20th April 1964, just a few weeks before I went to the interview that led to me becoming a 'Man of The Junction'. The 'cloud which wouldn't go away' is to be seen encroaching on the left in the form of a pair of Western Region DMUs alongside the magnificent Southern (and one Standard) steam locomotives arrayed outside roads 7 to 12.

Exmouth Junction shed in the summer of 1964, as it was when I became an Apprentice Fitter at the shed. On the left is the ominous form of a Western Region Diesel Multiple Unit whilst one of that Region's Pannier tanks, No.4655, is prominent on the left. No former Southern Railway designs are seen, the remainder being an ex-LMS Ivatt tank, another Pannier and four Standards The tenders show that at least two of these had spent their entire careers on the Southern Region, the one on the left page having a BR1F tender, like No.73112 'The Red Knight' which I saw here on 1st June 1964.
Photo: Amyas Crump collection.

wonder as we walked along, being careful not to trip over bits and pieces lying around, parts of engines of which I had no idea what they were or where they went. Amid the snatches of conversation describing which was which and what route it was used on, I wandered on in a daze and so to this day I can still only recall snatches of that afternoon.

The final part of the visit I do remember, and that was a talk given by a fitter on the then newly introduced AWS (Automatic Warning System) system then being fitted to the locomotives. It was an adaptation of the former GWR ATC (Automatic Train Control). After this we made our way out and to the bus stop just outside the depot. We caught the 'D' service to the city centre and then buses home, mine the No 9 to Sidmouth to alight in the middle of the country and a 1 mile walk home; in those days no one worried about their children walking home alone. Needless to say Mum and Dad were eager to hear about the trip. Little was I to know that it was to be the beginning of events that would lead to my involvement in the depot.

The year is now 1964 and I am preparing to leave school and enter the world of work. People from my generation left school at 15 and usually either took an apprenticeship or worked on the land, as many from my school came from outlying farms, and employment was fairly easy to get. So, after an abortive attempt with my parents preferring me to join the local gas company, I was free to pursue my own desire and so join the railway in Exeter.

Thus it was in May of 1964 that I applied for a job as a apprentice fitter with British Railways in Exeter. A letter arrived and I was asked to attend an interview at Exeter St David's station on May 30th at 2.00pm. My Mum, and I don't think she was unaware of what it meant to me, came along as Dad couldn't get the time off: again, it was then not unusual for a parent to attend an interview with their offspring.

Standing at the door of a dream and with it the possibility of it becoming a reality was not lost on me. The interview was warm and friendly, helped perhaps

A somewhat soft but nevertheless fascinating view from the top of the coal hopper looking towards Exeter with Exmouth Junction itself prominent near the top centre. The Southern's West of England main line runs from bottom left to top centre, the junction to the Exmouth branch diverging behind the white-roofed Exmouth Junction signalbox and running off to the left centre. Almost top dead centre is the 263 yard long Mount Pleasant (or Blackboy) Tunnel, which leads down to Exeter Central. To its right is the Exmouth Junction freight yard, and centre right is the famous concrete works, whose products were virtually the 'signature' of the Southern Railway. Finally, leading into the bottom right corner, are the access roads to Exmouth Junction Shed, the sloping roof being the covering to the water tower.
Photo: E Goff.

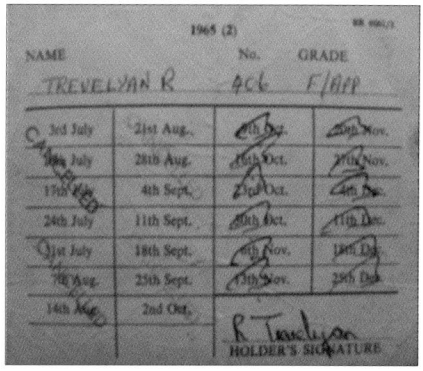

when it came out that my great grandfather had worked at Newton Abbot as a blacksmith and that my uncle was a station inspector at the same station. A job was offered, subject to the usual caveat of a successful medical, details of which would be notified later.

My joy knew no bounds and when asked if I had any questions, I enquired as to the possibility of visiting the depot at Exmouth Junction, in the Western Region since January 1963, on the following day, Saturday. A phone call was made to the shed master and with his agreement I was told to report to a Mr Smale about 11.00 in the morning.

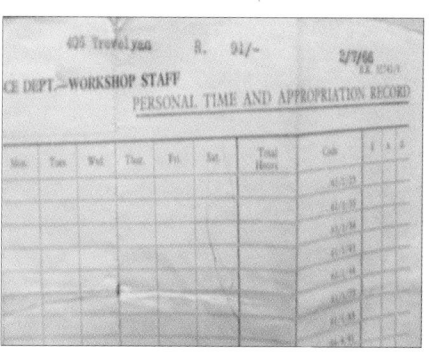

For my second visit it was a warm sunny day and with excited hearts my brother Peter and I set off for the bus to Exeter. We walked the two miles out to the suburb of Beacon Heath where the depot was situated, and, as the name implied, at the junction where the Exmouth branch left the main line. As we approached the sight and size of the depot again filled me with awe. Once more we ventured past the forbidding sign and into this cathedral of steam, and along the towering lifting road. Upon asking directions to the shed master's office, we were led to his door, ushered in and instructed to wait. With nerves tingling we waited for this man who possibly would hold my future in his hands. A tall individual entered wearing a trilby hat and, smiling, he introduced himself as Mr Smale the Shed Master. Following a brief talk, during which I was told that steam was on the way out, to be replaced by the new diesel-hydraulics that had already ousted steam from the railway down the hill, a cloud started to form in my otherwise perfect world.

Mr Smale arranged for a senior apprentice to show us around the depot, and as he led us out we stood at the top of the lifting road where we paused to look out across the depot yard where for the present at least steam reigned

almost supreme. Being a Saturday there were extra trains being run so several engines had come on shed and were being serviced by the coaling tower. Steam was issuing from everywhere, although I did note the presence of a couple of diesels. Our guide confirmed what we had been told earlier, that these would soon replace all that could be seen. I could not accept this, preferring to believe it would never happen and that things would stay as they were, for ever. Oh! - was I to learn the hard way!

We climbed into the cab of a D7000 Hymek diesel and I have to admit I was impressed by the layout and the cleanliness of it compared with a steam engine, however I still knew what I preferred. As we entered the depot proper, the sound of hammering, men shouting, drivers and firemen coming and going off duty was present, all to the background of issuing steam; it made the depot seem alive. Walking back down the lifting road we passed a BR Standard 4-6-0, No.73030, whose wheels had been removed, the apprentice told us that this was the last day of heavy steam repairs - with the depot full of steam engines it was again hard to believe. He led us around slowly taking care to explain what was going on and the various changes that would take place as well as answering my questions.

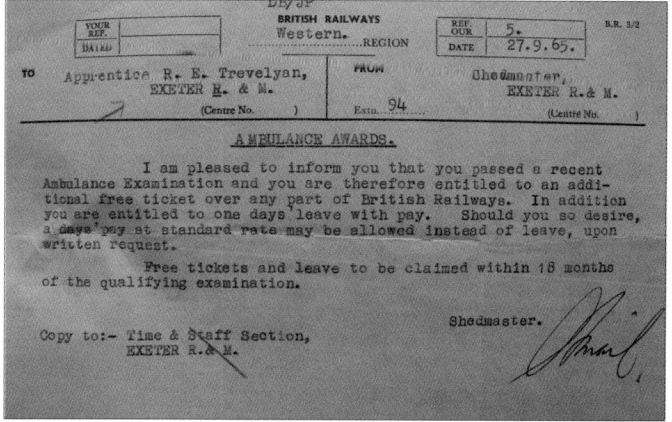

I wish I could remember his name, for he was a very good ambassador and guide. I must confess I didn't take everything in, as I will admit that I was too busy being a train spotter taking numbers down and looking for the unexpected. As we continued our tour, two ex-

Top to bottom: Wages ID card both sides, Work sheet on which to list jobs done for the week, Ambulance award letter.

11

GWR engines were pointed out, these were apparently there for possible snowplough duties especially after the winter the previous year when the country was gripped by the worst snowfalls since 1947. In addition there were Southern Region engines from Salisbury and London all waiting for their next duty, one in particular standing out, named BR Standard No. 73112 'The Red Knight', from Nine Elms in London.

We were taken to the back of the depot to watch an engine being turned and noticed that unlike the turntable at St David's this one was powered. We walked back through the depot and stood to take it all in, some engines sleeping some dozing others impatient to get going - it had been an amazing two hours but now it was time to take our leave so after a heartfelt "thank you" to our guide we walked back out and the 'D' bus. I looked around and pondered on what had been said. In my mind a perfect day was marred by the cloud which wouldn't go away.

Ex-GWR Collett 'Baby Castle' or 2251 class 0-6-0s Nos.2277 and 2214 in store for possible snowplough duties on 23rd January 1964.
Photo: Maurice Dart

***Below** is the plan for the first Exmouth Junction shed, opened in 1887. There is some disagreement between sources as to the exact size of the original turntable. Hawkins and Reeve describe it as 65' in the text accompanying the plan shown below which is taken from their book 'An Historical Survey of Southern Sheds' (OPC 1979) whilst others describe it as 55' when the shed was opened and replaced by a 65' one when the second shed was built. Information provided to me agrees with the latter. It appears that it was agreed that a 65' table was required in 1914 but it was not ordered until 1923 and thus installed as part of the new works.*

This first shed was built to a fairly standard LSWR design, both the building itself, the coal stage and the track layout with through roads feeding a turntable. Plymouth Friary is an example of this on a smaller scale. Eastleigh and Nine Elms were similar, as were Salisbury and Strawberry Hill, although the latter were dead-end sheds. These others all lasted much longer than Exmouth Junction's building, some to the end of steam, although by then most were in the state that Exmouth Junction reached before the First World War.

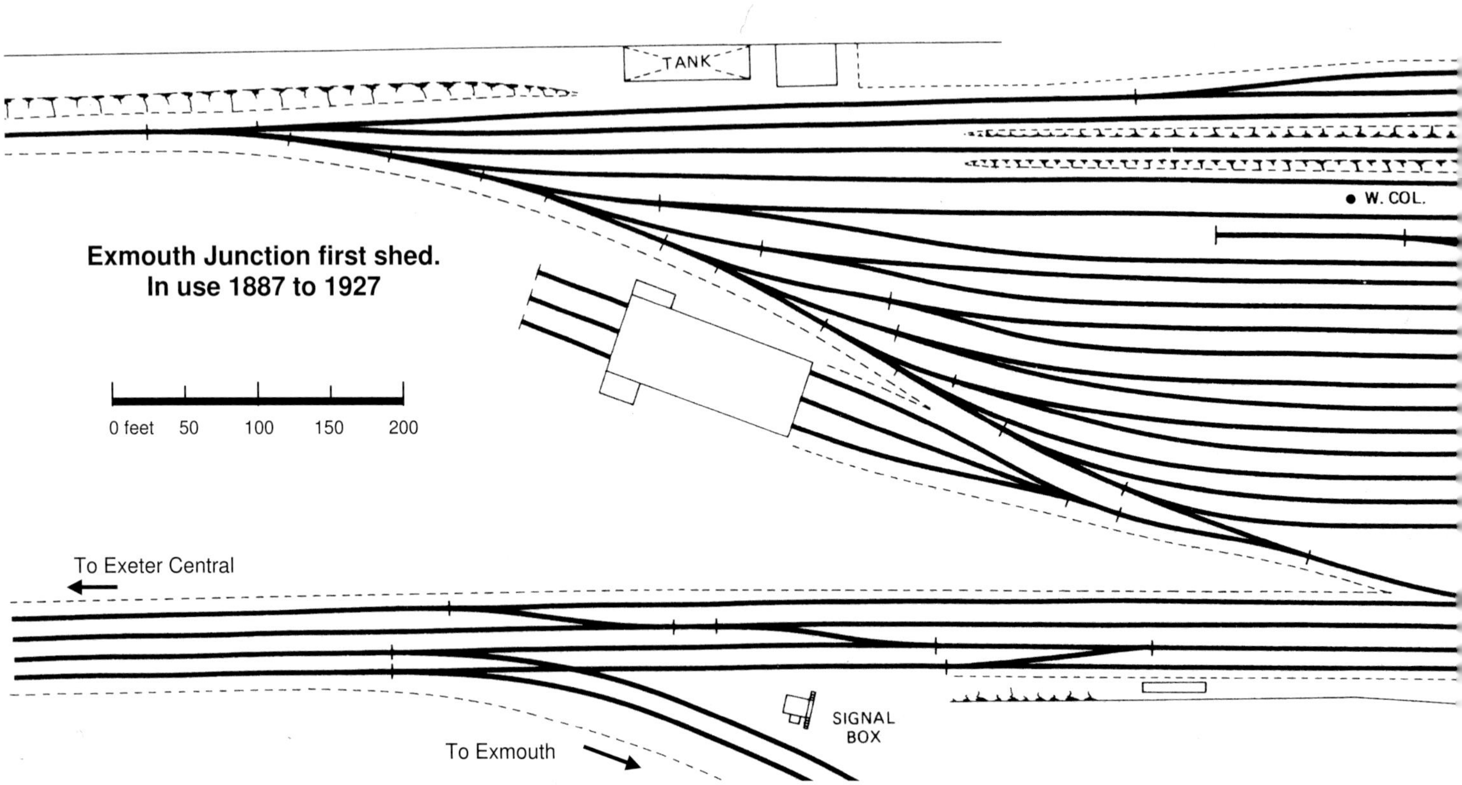

Exmouth Junction first shed.
In use 1887 to 1927

Chapter 2
A Short History of Exmouth Junction shed

In an area known as Beacon Heath, just outside Exeter, a piece of land that was once home to apple orchards, and bordered a former Priory, was bought in 1880 by the London and South Western Railway (LSWR). The reason for the purchase was to build a locomotive depot to replace the cramped and outgrown one at Exeter's Queen Street Station.

The soon-to-be-cleared area at Queen Street was later developed into a carriage shed, but the former depot offices were retained until 1967 as a signing-on point for loco crews picking up trains in the station. In today's atmosphere of green environmentalism, it is doubtful that permission for the brick, corrugated sheet and steel building would have been granted, but this was the 1880s and at the time the country was in the grip of expansionism, both at home and abroad. So a 225' x 165' shed was built, spanning 11 tracks and providing cover for 40 locomotives. A 55' turntable was also provided at the rear of the shed, along with a ramped, covered coal stage and a brick-built water tower - the latter was still present in 2012 - albeit minus the actual water tank.

Here at the depot, locomotives used for the expanding rail services to London, via Yeovil and Salisbury, to Plymouth, North Devon, North Cornwall and East Devon were serviced and maintained. The allocation then consisted of a motley collection of ancient locomotives, together with some of the new designs by Adams and, to be added later, engines from the Dugald Drummond and Robert Urie stable.

Over the next 40 years, the area became overrun with locomotives and the paraphernalia and debris associated with them. Thus the allocation outgrew the site, maintenance suffered and the buildings themselves deteriorated, especially after the Great War, so that their appearance became positively skeletal.

Things got so bad that, in 1922, the LSWR authorized a program of improvements, just before the great amalgamation, or Grouping, of the railways in 1923 which created, amongst others, the Southern Railway, which was to consist of the LSWR, LBSCR, IoWR and the SECR. These were to be put in hand to bring the railway's infrastructure into the 20th century and the Exmouth Junction shed (so called as it stood opposite the junction for the line from Exeter to Exmouth) was among those at the top of the list for complete renewal.

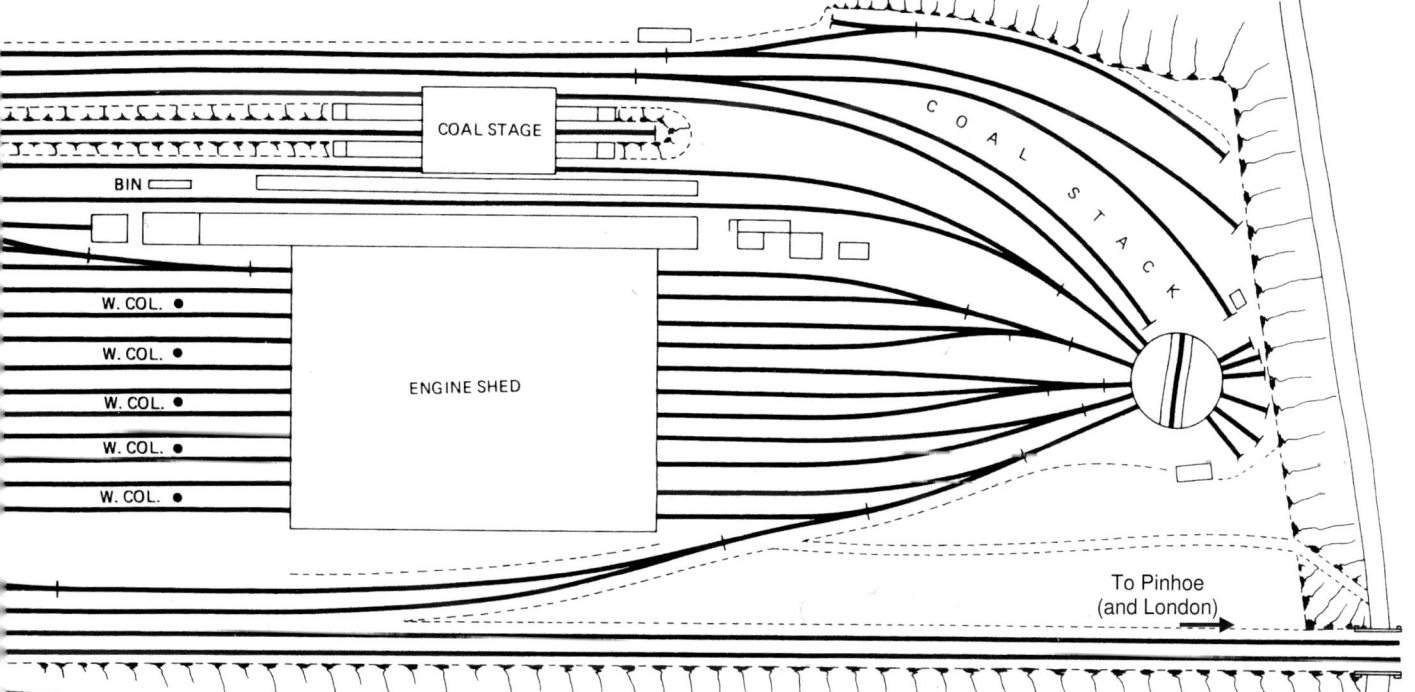

The first depot at Exmouth Junction. Completed in the late 1880s construction was far less solid than might appear from this image. Within a relatively short space of time the basic corrugated iron fabric had rusted away resulting in working conditions that were poor even for the period. On the extreme left the early carriage stock may well now be in engineers' use.

The rear of the original shed - the first depot was a through shed, the second and final shed, a dead-end - with the original 55' turntable visible. As early as 1914 this was considered too small and plans had been made for its replacement. In the event a 65' turntable was not installed until the second shed was built in the 1920s.

*The old order - by the time the Southern Railway was formed in 1923 the old shed was literally falling apart. By the time these two photographs were taken the 'Southern' livery had been applied to many locomotives and modern steam designs such as the Maunsell Moguls had been introduced to supplement the myriad 4-4-0s. In the view **above** one of the final survivors of William Adams' first type of 4-4-0, a member of the 380 class, nicknamed 'Steamrollers', the last of which, number 0162, was withdrawn from The Junction in late 1925, is seen alongside an N15 and an O2 still sporting its Adams stovepipe chimney and one of Drummond's 'Hopper' 4-4-0s, the mixed traffic version of the T9s. One of the latter, No.717 is seen - **below** - sandwiched between one of the N class moguls and another Adams locomotive, this time one of the 395 class 0-6-0s, three of which survived in service at Exmouth Junction until 1957/8.*

The design and materials for the replacement shed used were a total departure from the past using the new medium of reinforced concrete for the buildings, as was already being used at Feltham, South London. Concrete was, of course, produced at the adjacent Concrete Works which serviced the whole of the Southern and produced what is probably its most characteristic image, in the form of the famous 'Odeon' style stations of the inter-war period and every form of lineside and general railway structure imaginable.

Work began in 1924, the original estimate of cost being put at £1,500, to include the building up of the embankment to the rear of the original shed and a concrete raft to spread the load of the new shed. These supported reinforced concrete pillars, measuring 12" x 18". On top of these were placed further beams, topped off with a roof of the 'north-light' pattern fitted with smoke chutes, known as 'jacks', each of which ran the length of the twelve 249' shed roads. Each road had a deep inspection pit with drains to clear any water or oil from the locomotives.
Road No.1 housed the breakdown crane, Nos.2-5 were for general maintenance, Nos.6-9 for examinations, such as *Valves and Pistons* and *Periodicals* on the Bullied Pacifics, and Nos.10-12 for washing and maintaining boilers. On the north side of the main building was an additional road, known as the Lifting road: this was provided beside No.1 road. The building here reached 30' high including copious glass to allow in the maximum amount of light. Here was located the heavy-duty 50 ton overhead travelling crane, supplied by Herbert Morris, which traversed the length of the building. Understandably because of its height, this building was often referred to as 'The Cathedral'.

On this road locomotives could be lifted and the wheels removed for repair/machining using the large wheel lathe positioned at the end. Attached to the side of this road were the offices, stores, toilets/washing facilities, machine shop and mess rooms for the enginemen and fitting staff. On the south end, and attached to the end wall, was a coal furnace and sand dryer with additional rooms for the men who did boiler washouts and fire lighting. The furnace was known as the 'Hod' because the containers, used by the firelighters for the removal of the live coals for lighting-up locomotives after repair or boiler washouts, were shaped like those used by builders for carrying bricks.

The new shed, pictured after 1929, when it was finally completed. On the left is Drummond T9 4-4-0 No.709; then comes Salisbury's 'Eastleigh Arthur' No.449 'Sir Torre'; to its right 1927-built S15 No.824, what appear to be three Drummond locomotives inside the shed and, on the turntable road on the south side, a Maunsell N class mogul.

*The new order: **above** the second Bulleid Pacific, number 21C2 'Union Castle' was allocated to Exmouth Junction from Autumn 1942 until 1954 is seen alongside the new shed in 1954 whilst **below** a pair of the smaller 'Light Pacifics' of the 'West Country' class are seen on the same road, probably in 1946. The first 20 of the class were allocated to Exmouth Junction from new in 1945 to work the lines beyond Exeter which were forbidden to the larger 'Merchants'. The nearer of this pair, No.21C106 'Bude' was soon to star in the Locomotive Exchanges of 1948. The rear engine appears to be No.21C117 'Ilfracombe'.*

CARRIAGE & WAGON REPAIR SHED

COAL STACK

WEIGHBRIDGE

WATER TANKS

To Exeter Central

SIGNAL BOX

To Exmouth

N

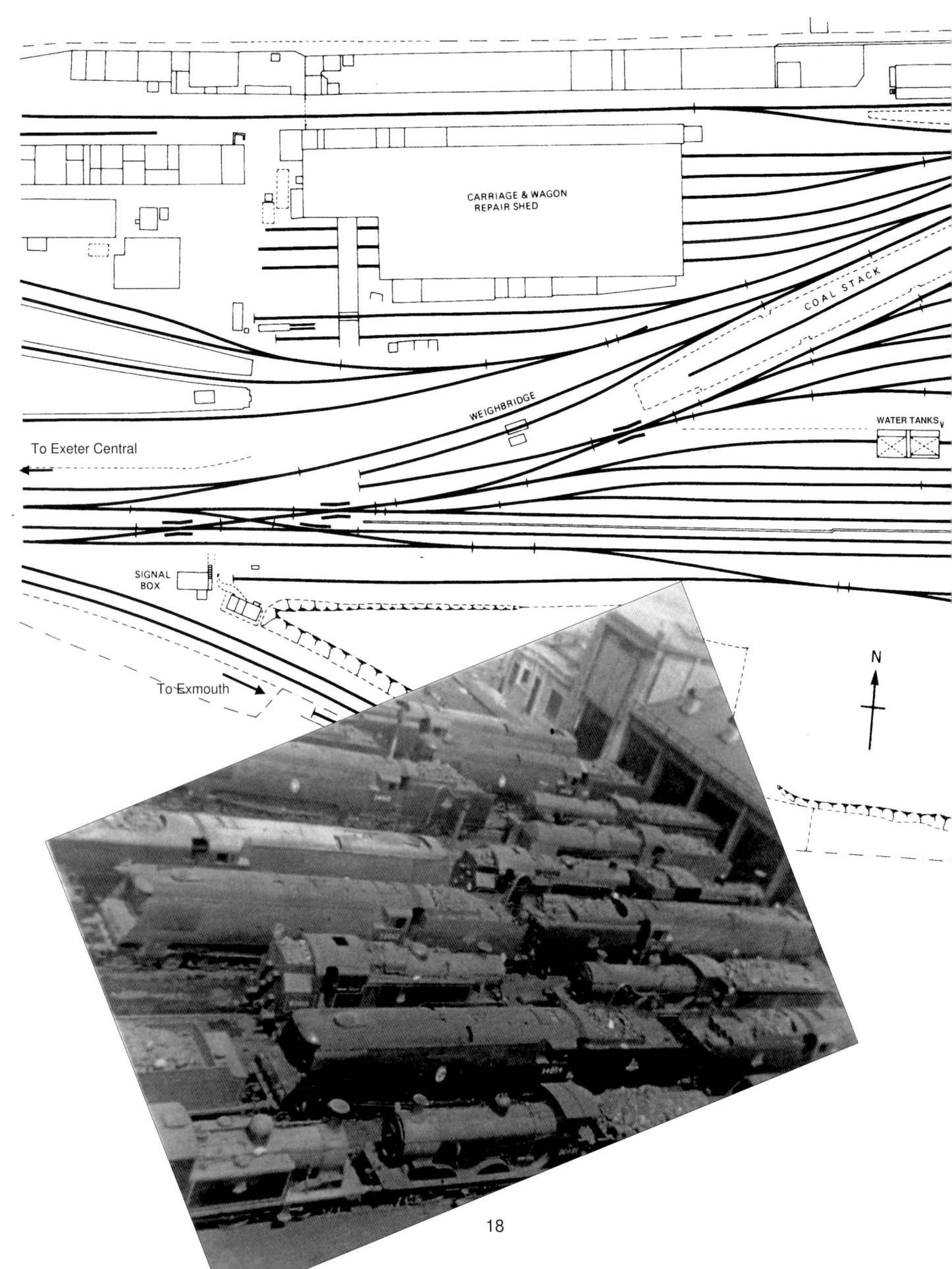

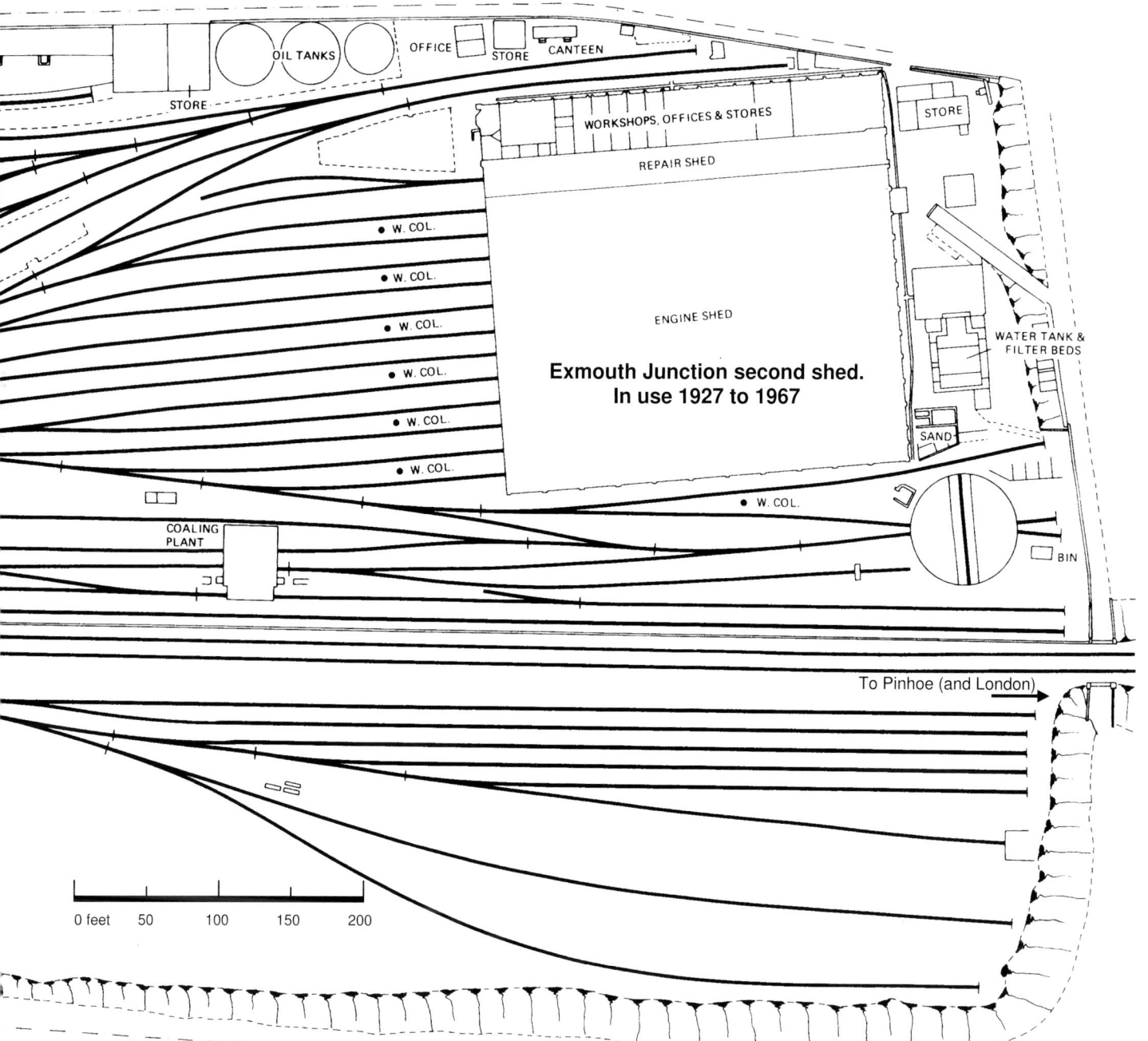

*Plan of the second Exmouth Junction shed (again courtesy of OPC) as remodelled between 1924 and 1929. The view **(left)** from the top of the coaling plant shows locomotives filling at least eight of the twelve shed roads during the 1955 ASLEF strike during which few trains ran. Three 'Merchant Navies' can be seen, 35001/2/3/4/8/13/23/24 being allocated to the Junction at the time. Five Light Pacifics, two U9s, two BR Standard 3 tanks, an N mogul, a 700, an M7 and an E1R complete the line-up and represent just 13% of the total allocation at the time. Reference to the plan will show that virtually every last foot of space must have been needed to store them all and also shows what a small proportion of the allocation is normally on shed.*

The angle of this view shows how difficult it was to obtain views such as this, but it emphasises the additional height of the 'Cathedral' or repair shed and lifting road by comparison with the main shed roads.

Photo: J Watts collection

The new shed together with the coaling monolith. In the 1930s some 110 engines were allocated here. Messrs. Reeves and Hawkins in their various excellent books on SR Engine Sheds, refer to how the detail design of the depot, albeit in concrete, was at least spared the bland appearance generally associated with this building material. For many years land surrounding the depot was primarily given over to farmland with only a few cottages nearby.

A mid-day view of the shed in the mid 1950s. The new high-mounted water tower and the full glazing on the end of the 'Cathedral' are the only obvious changes to the shed itself over a period in excess of a quarter of a century.

The locomotive stock, however, has undergone quite a few changes! Only the M7 and N classes are common to both photos, Bulleids and Standard tanks having ousted the Adams 4-4-0s, the N15s and the O2s seen in the upper view and on the previous pages.

Around the back and side of the shed ran a narrow gauge railway for the movement, from the stores, of heavier spares such as springs and large locomotive brake blocks. Just to the side of the sand-drying furnace a large water tower, standing 120' high and holding some 30,000 gallons, was erected, coming, it was said, second-hand from London. Underneath it, a series of filter beds, filled with wood wool, cleaned the outfall from the pits and separated the oil and water, the water being recycled to the tower above for high pressure boiler washing. Attached at the top of the tower was a signal arm used for sighting tests by the Locomotive Inspectors when examining the eyesight of footplate men whilst standing at the Mount Pleasant (or Blackboy) tunnel a quarter of a mile away. (A pre-arranged sequence of movements for signal sighting was organised by the inspector beforehand). Along the outside of the sand dryer was a new 65' turntable, replaced in 1947 by a 70' vacuum operated turntable (the term 'vacuum' meaning it used the loco's braking system) necessary to accommodate the very long-wheelbase Bullied Pacifics then being introduced into service; it could be hand operated if necessary. Perhaps the most modern of all the facilities provided was the coaling tower, before the arrival of which all coaling was done by hand. Built over two tracks, again using ferro-concrete, it was built by the Mitchell Conveyer Co., its bunkers holding 300 tons of coal. Man-handling was kept to a minimum with the installation of a wagon tippler which, by means of ropes and capstans, moved and hoisted the wagons to a height of 58' before these were turned over at a 60° angle at the top of the tower to empty the contents into the bunkers below. A sprinkler system was installed over the eight chutes to dampen the dust while coaling the locomotives. These towers were fine for the harder coal originally used but when softer coal was supplied in later years a considerable amount of dust was created as the coal broke up on falling into the hopper - it was advantageous to keep the bunker full to minimise this. During the 1940s a hood, provided to prevent dust escaping and contaminating the area, had the secondary advantage of also improving the appearance of the tower.

34080 '74 Squadron' moves off from the coaling tower on the coaling and disposal road in order to be turned on the turntable at the far end of the shed as another 'Light Pacific' waits to takes its place whilst an S15 takes water alongside the ash pits. The allocation of the Light Pacifics was fairly constant during their first decade, although the original intention of having 'West Countries' working in the West Country and 'Battle of Britains' working on the old South Eastern and Chatham lines went by the board, the second batch of 'West Countries' all going east whilst the first of the 'Battle of Britains' started life at Salisbury and were regular visitors to The Junction. 34080 initially went to Ramsgate but was transferred to Exmouth Junction at the beginning of 1958 and stayed until its withdrawal in September 1964.
Photo: E Crawforth.

Double-headers were unusual and normally discouraged on the Southern, but not completely absent. Here U class No. 31633 and an unidentified S15 pass Exmouth Junction signal box (its roof can just be discerned above the tender of the S15) on a down train on 27th June 1959. Photo: E Crawforth.

A hut for the Pointsman who controlled the approach and departure roads of the shed was situated at the throat of the depot. The shed yard was fitted with a Tannoy loudspeaker system (used by the Pointsman to call a locomotive forward ready for its departure time). Within this hut was a stove for warmth and a desk for recording each arrival and departure. The actual points were automatically sprung for the disposal and coaling roads although if a loco or the breakdown train arrived and needed to go straight on to one of the shed roads, the man on duty would have to hold the point over to allow it to pass. Being a premier depot, a full breakdown train was maintained, latterly this comprised a 45 ton Ransome and Rapier steam crane and a combined mess and tool van. Another such van was kept for breakdowns not requiring the crane. When the Civil Engineer's department was undertaking major engineering projects, the breakdown crane was often called upon to assist. This could be for bridge renewal or for other associated heavy lifting being undertaken throughout the West Country.

Former LSWR Lavatory Brake Third No. DS1809 built in February 1910 as LSWR No.1517 (SR No.2972) for one of the well-known 3-car sets used on cross-country and local services until the middle of the 1950s is seen on 19th July 1960.after a final spell of use as a Mess and Tool van for the Breakdown Train. It was thus converted in August 1953.
Photo: E Crawforth

Above - *Rebuilt Bulleid Pacific No.34053 'Sir Keith Park' on Salisbury duty 453 reverses to go on shed at Exmouth Junction in September 1959 after running light from Sidmouth Junction whence it had taken a through train to the Sidmouth and Exmouth lines from Waterloo.*   *Photo: E Crawforth.*

Below - *The pointsman's hut in BR days. (Exmouth Junction signal box, which controlled access in and out of the depot, is in the left background.) This is a latter day view as a former WR engine is included in the group.*

Just after the war (1947) a severe coal shortage resulted from the need to export as much of the best coal produced as possible to earn hard currency to pay back the crippling war debt. This was further exacerbated by the cruellest winter in living memory when around three months of sub-zero temperatures were endured. With the price of oil being very low, the Government planned to convert some of the steam stock to oil burning. Every Region was affected and, at Exmouth Junction, large oil tanks and a boiler house were built, supplemented by a 'D' class tank engine as back-up if the heating boiler failed. By the time this was implemented, circumstances had changed again and as the price of oil rose the whole project became surplus to requirements. Many of the locomotives which had already been converted returned to burning coal (some, all the oil-fired T9s for instance, went for scrap) and the project was abandoned, a colossal amount of money being wasted.

Ironically there was also only one converted loco based at the Junction, a 'U' class 2-6-0 tender loco. After a while the oil tanks were cut up for scrap and the boiler house eventually converted for the central heating system which was installed during the 1950s improvements. At the same time, and included in the improvements of the period, was the construction of a number of brick buildings at the rear of the shed. These comprised an Ambulance/First Aid room, a mess room for the maintenance workers, and next door, a store for boiler tubes, latterly converted into a workshop for the ODM (Outdoor Machinery) department which looked after the plant and equipment at the depot, as well as other depots and stations in the area.

Throughout the 1950s and for the first three years of the 1960s, Exmouth Junction remained the Southern Region's principal locomotive shed in the West Country. It had numerous sub-sheds, at Lyme Regis, Seaton, Sidmouth, Exmouth, Barnstaple Junction, Ilfracombe, Okehampton, Bude, and Wadebridge, being responsible for all locomotives sub-shedded in these outlying places. The lines beyond Exeter were known as the 'Withered Arm' and were difficult to work economically. The Southern had made no direct plans to streamline them or dieselise them by the time the whole of the Southern west of Wilton was passed into Western Region hands on 1st January 1963.

Almost the only modification at Exmouth Junction was the replacement, by 1962, of the water tank which had straddled the track by the ash pits by one to the side of the pits. Also several small huts were erected or replaced, most notable being the one beside the new water tanks which gave additional shelter for the disposal staff.

'Merchant Navy' No.35024 'East Asiatic Company' is given some remedial attention outside the repair shed in the early 1950s: the chimney has been removed and placed on the top of the casing! Behind it is one of the oil tanks installed for the ill-fated oil-firing project of 1947 whilst in the foreground are drums of oil used to fill the sumps of the original Bullied Pacifics. *Photo: RCTS CRA0156*

Above - A Rebuilt 'Merchant Navy' has its smokebox cleaned out by Philip Connelly in 1959. The original over-track water tower can be seen above the locomotive
Photo: W. Philip Connolly/Robert Humm coll'n

Left - On 8th March 1963 Standard class 4 tank No.80064 stands amid the ash on the disposal road alongside the new water tank replacing that which used to straddle the track here .

Photo: E Crawforth

Down and out. **Above -** *Withdrawn in September 1964, Nos.34096/31845/31406 are lined up ready to see their maker in the down sidings on the 6th of that month.* **Below -** *The final insult: WR DMUs and Hydraulics take over.*
Photos: above: E Crawforth, below: Bob Tacagni

The Western soon introduced modernisation, initially by the substitution of their own steam locomotives for the ex-Southern ones it had acquired, which were soon returned to Eastleigh. Diesel refuelling equipment was installed during 1964 and the outside lighting improved. That was the beginning of the end. With the loss of its steam allocation in 1965 and the end of servicing facilities for incoming steam locos from other depots in 1966, several of the water cranes outside the shed had their hoses/bags removed. The turntable, wheel lathe, large water tower (at the rear of the shed) and useful metal from the coal hopper were removed during the summer of 1966.

Formal closure of Exmouth Junction came on 6th March 1967. A long-fought campaign, which included a march to Downing Street to hand in a petition, was all to no avail. Ironically, another refurbishment had been scheduled to take place to further adapt the depot for diesel work, this having been agreed only days before the eventual closure. Subsequently the Carriage and Wagon Department used roads 11 and 12 for repairs to 21 ton coal wagons as they had run out of space in the main building, but it was short lived. A similar short term arrangement was by the ODM, which had by then moved back to the C & W area, also occasionally using the lifting road for repairs to the wheel sets of track maintenance machines. After a short time all had ceased and the depot quickly fell into decay.

The tracks were lifted during 1968/9 and the buildings demolished during the summer of 1970, the massive concrete coal hopper being blown up during October of that year. After this the site was left empty, until the local Co-op bought part of the land and built a retail store during the early 1980s. Since then, in 2012, the Carriage and Wagon site has been cleared and the area has been partially integrated by Morrison's, who now own the Supermarket, to create a new fuel station and additional parking. A note of interest whilst clearing the land is that the original shed pits were uncovered revealing the floor being of inlaid brick.

The last chapter, the coal hopper awaits demolition in October 1970. The site had been a steam shed for just over 80 years, the time split almost equally between the old and new sheds.

During the few minutes lay over at Salisbury, two Salisbury men shovel coal forward on the tender of a 'Pacific', working a West of England service. The fireman in the meanwhile has the slightly easier task of replenishing the tender tank. Salisbury shed came within the Exmouth Junction district until the regional boundary changes of the early 1960s. The depot at Salisbury was second in importance to Exmouth Junction in the West of England.

Chapter 3
Men of The Junction

One can only imagine what it was like for the men in 1929 as they moved from the old derelict depot that was falling apart around them, to the new, clean concrete building with all its modern conveniences.

The offices were bright, with good window space, they were heated and lit by electricity, the mess rooms had gas cookers and the washrooms running hot water, flushing toilets - *inside* the building: many men didn't even have this at home! For the maintenance staff the immediate improvement was that it was dry, with plenty of light coming through from the glass roof panels. They had purpose-built tool cupboards and work benches for each fitter and boilersmith, and in the large and airy machine shop a lot of the machines were modern with self contained power units. Admittedly shafting was installed for the older machines brought in from the old shed, and there was a blacksmith's hearth and facilities for remetalling bearings and presses for removing and refitting of bushes, but the main improvement for the fitting staff was the lifting road. There were no hand cranes, jacks and packing here - instead, an electrically driven overhead crane with more than sufficient strength for lifting engines from their wheels.

With such surroundings morale could only ever be high. They now had a depot to boast of, the largest and most modern in the West Country so, yes, it was going to be the best in every way. From the District Motive Power Superintendent down to the lowly shed labourer all were proud when asked where they worked, "Up Junction" they'd reply. Everyone in the area understood what they meant and many were secretly jealous, for in those days the railway was a job for life: you started at 14/15 and expected to stay until 65. Of course things changed over the years, but not the pride of working at a premier depot and this carried on to the end in 1967. If you talk today with any of the retired staff who worked there, that sense of pride still comes across.

Even during the dark days of the 1940s the pride shone through. Men of Exmouth Junction pose on and in front of an old Adams class O2 0-4-4 tank. Dating back to 1890 No.181 would be 'exported' to the Isle of Wight in April 1949 as that system's No.W35 and be named 'Freshwater', in which guise it would last until October 1966 when steam finished on the island.

To fully understand what it was like we have to talk with the men, going back to the time, fixed forever in their memories, and again detect the thrill of signing on ready to start the day's or night's work. You may think by today's standards it's fanciful thinking - surely nobody was that happy, nobody cared that much for work or colleagues? But you'd be wrong: read on and be prepared to catch the flavour and see what I mean, be prepared to let yourself be transported back to those days and then tell me I'm wrong. Let me introduce you to them: from the 'Guv'ner' to the newest apprentice, they were all 'Men of The Junction'.

District Locomotive Superintendent

Mr A W Johnston was the District Locomotive Superintendent during the time of Southern Region control. The area that he covered was known as the Exeter Motive Power District and, in terms of areas, was the largest in the whole of the Southern Region. Exmouth Junction was therefore the natural, as well as the biggest and most central, base in the district, Salisbury was second, followed by Yeovil, Plymouth, Barnstaple and Wadebridge. The headquarters office was originally next door to the shed master but was later moved to a purpose-built office situated across from the main building by the access lane. Mr Johnston oversaw all of the sheds under his control, liaising with the Exmouth Junction shed master who was in effect his deputy. Mr Johnston was the one who set in motion the directives received from Regional Headquarters at Waterloo and from the main works at Eastleigh. He made sure that the local shed master understood and followed the orders and, when necessary, got involved in the negotiations with the local union representatives. Mr Johnson was known to have been a fair man and considerate towards the staff under his care.

Shed Masters

It is interesting to note that the practice on the Southern was to promote men from the Mechanical side to the position of shed master and this was applied to all sheds within the Exeter District. For example, Claud Dare, a charge hand from the junction, was promoted to Salisbury whilst others went to Plymouth Friary and to Wadebridge. Listed below are the men who held the post of shed master during the period 1939-1967:

1939-1942 Eddie Hoare; 1942-1947 Mr Steel; 1947-1953 Mr Rogers; 1953-1956 S Webster; 1956-1957 E S Beavor.

The last named, while still being mechanically trained, broke tradition by coming from the Eastern Region, where he had been one of Sir Nigel Gresley's pupils. He was well liked and, one of the benefits of new blood, brought new ideas to the depot. He also saw to it that the maintenance staff had the most up to date equipment. However, his term was short lived; coming in the January of 1956 he stayed for only just over a year before taking a post at Waterloo with the Work Study department in November 1957. As previously noted, he later wrote two books about his working life on the railway, including his time at the Junction. These were *Steam Was My Calling* and *Steam Motive Power Depots*, each a worthwhile read for those who wish to know more of the intricate details involved in working with steam Locomotives.

1957-1962 H Moore.

Mr Moore had been the Mechanical foreman at the Junction for many years so was well known around the depot. A kindly man, he was very much of the old school, was fair but did not suffer fools gladly.

1962-1966 Charlie Smale.

Mr Smale had arrived at Exmouth Junction, with several others from Ashford, as a fitter during the war. He subsequently rose through the ranks until he became mechanical foreman, replacing Mr Moore. Unfortunately by the time he took over as shed master the stature of the role had diminished greatly, not least as by this stage the shed was under Western Region control from the Plymouth District office.

1966-1967 R Meggett (Area Maintenance Engineer Exeter).

This was a new post and title which not only covered the new diesel depot but also the Plant and Machinery, Carriage and Wagon and the Road Motor Engineers Departments in Exeter.

Locomotive Inspectors

Sam Smith, Edgar Snow, Charlie Rooke.

The duties of the locomotive inspectors, also referred to as footplate inspectors, were varied but concentrated on the development and nurture of the footplate crew. A good inspector was one who remembered from whence he himself had come and sought only the best for, and from, those under him. In the pecking order they stood between the shed master and the running foremen. It was their task to undertake the training of the young cleaner and examine him according to the rule book and his knowledge of the locomotive. This continued as the man developed into a fireman and then (hopefully) a driver, each exam being harder and more thorough, so that by the time the drivers position was reached the individual would know the rule book inside out and be conversant with every part of the locomotive. Many Inspectors organised, and in their spare time ran, Mutual Improvement Classes, the premises and equipment used being supplied by the railway. Sam Smith also wrote a small handbook for footplate men, his own son becoming a fitter at the shed.

Running Foremen

The job of a Running Foreman was not, as the name might imply, running around chasing men to make sure their jobs were done properly, but making sure that those under his care - the drivers, firemen and cleaners - were doing their jobs as laid down, so that the shed was seen to operate smoothly. This meant knowing where locomotives were, what duties were involved and when engines and men were due out (and due in), including where the men were so that he could be sure that every crew went out with the right engine and on time.

Jack Tilley was just such a man who, by the time I knew him, had been a Running Foreman for many years. Originally, like the other foremen, he had been through the footplate grades, from cleaner to driver and then on to be a 'Runner' or assistant. Jack had an encyclopaedic mind able to remember drivers, their turns and the relevant notices from having read them only once. He was also always ready to offer assistance to anyone who needed it, be it footplate staff or others in the depot. He would, when needed, go into the messroom to arrange a specific job. On one occasion, Jack walked in and, after selecting a crew, told them to go to Yeovil with empty wagons and come home 'light engine', saying, "…and I want that engine back for the 6.30 am Waterloo". After pausing for breath he added firmly, "And make sure you bring it back!" Nobody minded because they knew he was doing it in their interests and he knew their job inside out. Jack never seemed to stay still, always busy about the place, and when in his office he seldom sat down. He was a man of action, his pipe, whether lit or not, always seemed to be in the side of his mouth and it would stay safely out the way as he shouted his commands from the other side! He maintained very good relations with the charge-hand fitters and the fitting staff as well as the charge-hand boilersmith. Together, they always made sure that, somehow, the right loco was always available to work the right train. A valued member of the First Aid team, he could be seen at most of the competitions and was always supportive when not needed to take an active part.

Ray Down was one of life's gentlemen, always smiling and gentle of voice. Where Jack was the 'hare', Ray was the 'tortoise', not that he was lazy or slow. On the contrary, he was every bit in charge and as conscientious as Jack was, certainly on top of the job. Like Jack, Ray cared and always had a kind word for anyone including train spotters, of which there where many in the late 1950s and 60s as steam was drawing to a close and the older classes were disappearing. There has been the idea that footplatemen and the maintenance staff did not get on but nothing could be further from the truth, certainly at 'The Junction'. As far as I can tell from my own observations, and comments from others, both sides knew it was in their best interests to get along and share information. As in all walks of life there are bound to be differences but, in the majority of cases, people like Ray fostered good relations: it was a privilege to have known them.

Bert Bufton, a Western Region man, came up from the shed at St Davids when it had closed in October 1963. At that time he had been in charge of the shed as acting shed master with the care of all staff as well as the footplatemen. Despite his background, which might have been expected to cause friction, he got on well with incumbent SR staff - no mean feat when there was still rivalry between the regions.

Other Running Foremen

There were many other foremen working as well: Dick Tilley (1908-1956), Fred 'Brocky' Brock and Alf Yelland, the latter a man with abilities similar to those of Jack Tiley. With a depot working 24 hours, 7 days a week, they needed to be on top of the job. There were also relief foremen known as 'Runners' who stood ready to fill last minute gaps in the roster, covering sickness and holidays. These were senior active drivers, usually from the main links, one of whom was Albert Watts, whose father had been a top link driver.

Running Foreman Ray Down, a lovely man - his face says it all! Photo: Ted Gosling/Mike Clements collection.

Office and Stores

Attached to the offices of the shed master and running foreman, the main office was ably run in the 1950s by, in turn, Horace Martin, Fred Purton and Gordon Tilley. There was also a roster clerk, Fred King, whose duties were to arrange the enginemen's duties. These were worked out to the finest detail so that every train booked off was allocated a turn number and all eventualities were taken into consideration. Thus when a man came on duty he knew what turn he was on and what the latest variations were. The office also catered for the wages of the one thousand or so staff employed at the height of the shed's existence during the 1950s. Other duties involved in those pre-computer days included assessing the welfare of the men, typing memos, the daily rosters of course, letters for all departments, organising leave and supplying the free travel passes. The railways were always very paper orientated, copies of everything having to be made and filed. Neither was the office always a male-only environment, as post-war there were several young female typists.

The stores were in-between the offices, messroom and the workshop, with rail access at the rear for unloading items from designated vans which arrived from Eastleigh Works. As befitted a main depot, the stores were large and carried everything needed to keep the locomotives running: from cotton waste to oil, nuts and bolts, piston rings, brass components such as injectors, clack valves and safety valves, 'H' and 'K' type vacuum ejectors and much more besides.

Due to the number of classes allocated or likely to visit the depot, a vast amount of stock was carried. This also meant some parts lay unused for years, until an inventory was taken and the decision made to regularly send someone in to sort it out with the surplus being returned to Eastleigh. Undertaking this task in the 1950s was Fred Purton, who moved from the main office, then in the 1960s the job was done by Ken Larcombe. Ken was brother in law to the Watts family who numbered a top link driver, a guard, a fitter and another driver in the immediate family!

Ken left no one in any doubt that he was in charge and woe betide anyone who tried to work around him. As an apprentice I found him to be fair and, so long as you respected his position and treated him accordingly, there was no problem. On the other hand, try to be clever and you got nothing unless it was in writing and duly signed. He oversaw a clerk and three stores issuers, the latter working a three shift system. These were the ones you approached initially at the main window, and as long as the right 'bit of paper' was given in, they, in their turn, issued what you had asked for. There were exceptions, such as cleaning cloths and cotton waste, etc, these were freely handed over the counter. With the cleaning cloths, dirty ones had to given in, whenever possible, in exchange for the clean items. When a driver or fireman was preparing a loco they would obtain tools (supplied in a bucket), oil, route discs or lamps and any other item required from the stores by giving the turn or locomotive number. Everything needed to keep the depot working was in the stores and jealously guarded by Ken and his stores issuers. The latter were a mixed bunch, some ex-footplatemen, others having moved from the lower grades in the shed, but all characters in their own right and usually helpful.

The Watts family gathering on the retirement of father Albert in 1964. Left to right (Brother) Bernard (Guard), son Albert (Driver), son-in-law Ken Larcombe (Stores), Frank "John" (Fitter) and Father Albert Snr (Driver).   Photo: J Watts collection

Locomotive Enginemen

It used to be every young boy's dream to be an engine driver. Many a lad would stare up at a steam engine as it arrived at the station, the driver and fireman busy, and imagine himself in their place. However, reality was different. You started as a cleaner, the work hard and dirty. Promotion was also slow, simply as most men wanted to stay at their local shed and not move away. On other regions the *only* way to get promotion was to move away, otherwise the only way on to actual footplate work was after several years being on shed, cleaning and running errands. As an example there were, at one time, 47 cleaners on the books at Exmouth Junction.

Eventually, having gained promotion from cleaner to passed-cleaner, the individual would at last be allowed off shed in the company of a driver or passed fireman. One can only imagine the joy of the first trip out, eager to please, mistakes invariably made but, with an understanding mate, this was all part of the learning curve. Each driver or fireman was an individual although, to the untrained eye, they might all appear to be the same. However, the differences were there, in the slant of the hat, perhaps the style, some not even wearing the regulation grease-top cap, preferring to replace these with cloth caps. Overalls too were worn differently, some done up to the neck while others left buttons undone to accommodate red or white neckerchiefs. Some wore the Edwardian style jacket, others an old sports jacket. It was the same with the firemen, the younger ones wore their cap set at a jaunty style, with the sides sewn down 'Guards' fashion, and polished. Often in a station with pretty girls around they would remove the cap and, with a swift run through with a comb, aim to impress by showing their 'Brylcreem'-covered hair to best advantage. Once on the move, the cap was replaced - to keep that precious hair free from coal dust and soot!

Footplate work was divided into 'Links', the top one being the 'Main Line', the preserve of senior drivers and firemen. A man often had to wait until his late forties before he would be promoted to the link. Theirs was a restricted route, principally the Exeter to Salisbury express and local passenger trains. The others were fairly self explanatory: the 'North Devon', the 'North Cornwall', the 'Plymouth', the 'Exmouth', and then the 'Black' gang, the last named for the freight trains that ran during the night, hence the name. After this was the 'Bank' link, which, as might be expected, covered the main banking duties involving two or three locomotives used for pushing (and sometime pulling) trains from St Davids station up the 1 in 37 bank through the tunnel to Exeter Central station. This same 'bank' link had the Exeter Central pilot/shunting engine amongst its turns. Banking a passenger train was usually just with one engine at the rear, but freights needed two and sometimes three, one on the front and two behind. This occurred mainly on the Meldon ballast train and later, during the 1960s, the Westbury to Exeter Central cement train. It was quite a sight to see one of these trains blasting away up the bank, especially at night, fiery red sparks thrown from the chimneys lit up the night sky. Further down came the spare links, the 'Senior spare' and after that, the lowest, the 'Junior spare'. These last links, the largest at the shed, covered anything from freight to mainline work and all else in between, and if there was nothing else, the men would be found preparation and disposal tasks.

Another duty essential to the running of the depot was that of the shed turner, performed by men who, for various reasons, were no longer allowed to drive beyond the shed limits. Under direct orders from the running foremen, they moved the locomotives from the disposal area to the coal hopper and then the turntable, positioning engines where they were needed and also shunting the stores vans when required. If the turner was not available then the duty spare men were allocated to the task.

There was a very strong union presence at The Junction, led by ASLEF. For many years, this was headed up by Leslie Lodge, a driver: his brother Charlie was another depot driver. Les served for many years on Sectional Council No.2, the Locomotive men's representative body at regional level and as such, according to E S Beavor in his book *Steam Was My Calling,* in some ways he carried more weight than a senior Shed Master - referring to himself. One can only imagine the diplomacy needed to keep things sweet! The other unions represented were the NUR and TESSA. Later on, several of the fitters became members of the AUEW but it was ASLEF that ran the shed, for without them, nothing moved. This went back to the days when drivers and firemen were considered as the elite and were consequently treated as such. Certainly at Exmouth Junction it must be said that, as far I know, they never purposely abused their position, but they did look after their members well!

Beavor goes on to say that the depot had a fine team spirit, which made management much easier than in many of the Midlands and Northern industrial areas where there was fierce competition for labour.

Incidentally it was the disastrous National Strike of 1955, lasting 17 days, that ultimately led to the decline of the railways, coupled with indifferent post-war Government support that further exacerbated it. The railways never recovered and continued to lose traffic until privatisation came in the 1990s.

With over 100 sets of men, it is impossible to include everyone, so a list of enginemen known to have worked at the junction is given later as an appendix.

No.35013 'Blue Funnel' under the coal hopper at 'EJ', being prepared for the up 'Atlantic Coast Express'.
Photo: Mark Abbot

As an idea as to the lives of those who worked on the footplate, I have included the testimonies of just two of them.

Edward 'Smokey' Crawforth was born into a railway family, his father being a guard based at Wallington and West Croydon in Surrey, the outskirts of suburban London. Many a time young Ted joined him on his duties and, if challenged, his Dad would just say "He's with me", and that was enough. Together they travelled over much of the Southern's Central Division, so hardly surprising that during this time a love for the railway began to show itself. But not for Ted the flags and lamps and riding at the rear of the train, no, for him it had to be up front on the footplate. So in 1951 he joined the railway, but as he was not old enough for footplate duties (he was not yet sixteen) he started at Wallington and West Croydon station as a junior porter.

On the 8 September 1952 he applied for the post of Engine Cleaner at Norwood Junction. Because of the state of recruitment in the area (less dirty jobs in other industries being readily available) promotion was rapid. He was soon passed to become a fireman and would have progressed further had not a holiday in Devon intervened. A visit to Exmouth Junction shed opened his eyes to the possibilities of working in a large shed, with an equally large operational area. So on returning he immediately applied for a transfer to The Junction but first had to do his National Service: in those days every eighteen year old lad had to do two years in one of the three services. After Ted's spell in the army he waited another two years before he was able to move, by which time he was also on the verge of becoming a Driver. However, such was the pull of working in Devon that he forewent that opportunity and instead opted to move to the South-West. On the morning of 15th June 1959, after an overnight journey aboard the 1am newspaper train from Waterloo, he walked to Exmouth Junction where he reported to the Running Foreman, Jack Tiley, and was introduced to Horace Moore the shed master.

Asked if he had ever worked on the Western Section, Ted replied, "No, only the Central". Mr Moore outlined the duties, the area and the locos he would work on, after which he told Ted that he had better spend the rest of the day looking for lodgings. When Ted replied, "I've found some, thank you sir", Mr Moore asked the question again. Ted's brow began to furrow, "Yes, I have some, thank you sir", came a somewhat hesitant reply this time, only for Mr Moore to repeat the question yet again. Now the penny dropped and he did indeed spend the rest of the day 'looking for lodgings'.

Ted's Drivers: *from top to bottom:*

Driver R Dack on class 700 0-6-0 No.30796 on duty 500, the 3.20pm Exeter Central to Yeovil 3rd September 1960.

Driver Ron Jury on Standard class 3 tank No.82023 approaching Exton on duty 616 on 22nd July 1959.

Driver Maurice Bevan with LMS Ivatt class 2 tank No.41320 on the last steam train to Lyme Regis on 2nd November 1963.

A thoughtful Driver Frank Churchill on N class mogul No.31838 working duty 586, the 9.55am stone empties from Exmouth Jct to Meldon Quarry on 28th December 1962.

All Photos: Ted Crawforth

Bright and early the following morning Ted made his way to the shed, his spirits high and his hopes even higher as he scrunched over the cinder path leading to the shed. Here was the fulfilment of his long awaited dream. Feeling as proud as punch, but not showing it, he walked through the entrance of the shed, past the Leading Fitter's office on the left, around the Mechanical Foreman's office on the right, past the huge wheel lathe and the lifting road and reported to the Running Foreman for his first duties as a junior fireman. It would be relevant to say at this point that most of the staff here were local men, coming from long-standing railway families and, as will be seen later, fathers worked with sons, and nephews with uncles. So for a 'London boy', as anyone emanating from east of Salisbury would be called here in what was a tightly knit community, he would need to exercise care so as not to blot his copybook straight away. Fortunately Ted understood this and so trod carefully during those first days. He succeeded as well, becoming a valued friend and workmate, fully accepted during his time, so much so that he still comes down to the annual November reunion at the Exmouth Junction Railway club in Whipton, Exeter.

During those first days in the spare link or gang he was prepared to do whatever was required: preparing or disposing work, joining the yard shunter or going down to Exeter Central station to bring back a loco or shunt the yard there. A month later, he joined the Exmouth gang, which involved duties over the Exeter to Exmouth, Exmouth to Sidmouth and Sidmouth Junction branches.

Ted worked with many drivers and enjoyed teamwork with the vast majority; he took photos of those with whom he particularly got on, men like Bob Dack, Ron Jury, Maurice Beavan, and Frank Churchill. When working with Frank he said that if he had a spare moment he would always clean the back of the boiler, with oil soaked cotton waste. The reason is not clear although it is known that, in the old days, the drivers expected their firemen to keep the footplate clean - not easy when one considers the conditions.

'SMOKEY'
(Ted Crawforth)

Ted on the footplate of one of the legendary Adams Radial Tanks that were retained at Exmouth Junction to work the tortuous Lyme Regis branch until 1962. No.30583 was working the Lyme Regis branch on 12th July 1960.

Photo: Ted Crawforth

It was now that he gained his nickname, 'Smokey', from the event about to be described. Whilst firing a BR Standard 2-6-2 tank on a light engine duty to Sidmouth Junction he was building up the fire, ready to start shunting when they arrived. But on the way and after a final shovelful on the fire, he noticed the distant signal for Whimple, a few miles before their destination, was 'on', meaning slow down and prepare to stop. Driver Ern Barribal duly shut off steam and with the fire doors closed and no draft of any consequence on the fire plus a firebox loaded with 'green' coal, a lot of smoke was pouring out of the chimney. Noticing this, the driver quickly turned on the blower to clear the smoke. Opening the firedoor, he looked at Ted and said, "what a smokey joe you are - look at it". Ted looked and saw a stream of black smoke stretching back a quarter of mile!

As they approached the signal box at Whimple, the signalman called out, "Who's sending up the smoke signals?" "My mate", shouted the driver, "he's from London, a proper smokey he is": not surprisingly the name stuck ever after. A year later on the 13th of June he joined the junior spare link, which meant covering for any duty, as required. It could be firing a freight to Barnstaple or Plymouth, or the Meldon Quarry stone trains, relieving on the various branch's or even a Waterloo express, plus shed work, such as disposing etc. This more or less continued until the end of steam. It was never boring as the turns were so varied that he would sometimes go for weeks before doing the same job again, whilst during the summer there was holiday relief at the outstation depots, Lyme Regis in particular, which meant lodging away.

Talking to Ted nowadays and more than 40 years after closure, the joy of working 'up the Junction' still comes across. It seems that nothing ever seemed too much trouble, neither the work nor conditions overwhelmed him and because of the family atmosphere it was a home from home. In 1981, Ted wrote a series of articles for *Railway World*, detailing some of his experiences whilst working at The Junction. These appeared in the February and July issues under the title 'Chronicles from Exmouth Junction'; a further article was published in September 1982. All are strongly recommended as they give a more detailed account of his time there. With Ted's permission I have included in the following Chapter 6 a previously unpublished article relating a trip on the Meldon ballast train from Exeter to Salisbury.

For many years Ted was involved with the Bluebell Railway, and also as a member of the Merchant Navy Locomotive Preservation Society he has spent a lot of time helping to keep No.35028 *Clan Line* going. He still retains a lively sense of humour and remembers (during the change over from steam to diesel) writing out a repair card for No.D826, *Intrepid,* saying 'Boiler keeps locking out - wish to point out did not have this trouble with 34026 *Yes Tor* yesterday'. With the closure of the depot, he, together with the other remaining staff, moved to Exeter St David's; he got married in the September and then returned east to Dorking in December 1967. His subsequent career was varied, being moved about as depots closed or were amalgamated. He retired early in 1995 and now lives at Felpham near Bognor Regis with his wife Freda, known affectionately as 'Blossom'. When talking to Smokey today, one still gets that feeling of the hairs rising on the back of the neck as he tells of his firing days. He refers to a series of dairies that he kept throughout his footplate career where every turn, driver and engine/train were recorded. No embellished stories here, just facts used as an aid to the memory. It would be impossible to experience such a life today, compared with his time the railways have changed out of all proportion, the last of the old generation almost all now being retired.

'Smokey' at Sidmouth Junction in 1959, where he got his nickname.

Photo: E Crawforth.

Now for a local lad, **Edward 'Eddie' Goff**. Eddie started in 1955 as a cleaner under the charge of one Bill 'Chopper' Caldicott, a character if ever there was one. As at other depots the duties of a cleaner were not restricted to just cleaning and preparing a locomotive for they were often required to go out and undertake callout duties: notifying drivers and firemen of any alteration to their booked duties. When engaged on cleaning, the first locomotives to be treated were those for mainline duty, then those on secondary passenger duties, such as the M7 (and later the BR Class 3) tanks, and, if after that there was sufficient time, any other loco that was spare on the depot.

Whenever a locomotive was being worked on, either by cleaner or maintenance staff, a 'Stop Board' had to be attached to the engine in question and under no circumstances was it to be moved. Eddie steadily rose through the ranks and became a passed cleaner and then a fireman, starting in the Junior Spare gang before joining the Exmouth gang where his regular mate was Frank Churchill. Eddie says of his twelve years on the railway that they were the best of his working life. He was known to be one of the cleanest fireman on the depot, he would arrive clean and even after eight hours work on the footplate would return home as clean as when he started. This came about after spending time working with Frank who behaved the same way, which in turn set an example for Eddie (and many others). He retained this smartness long after leaving the railway.

In trying to remember his time, and the events he experienced, Eddie recalled the terrible winter of 1963, while travelling from Okehampton on a West Country Pacific when they ran into a snowdrift as high as the locomotive. Once clear, another job involved them clearing snow by hand from point gaps to avoid being derailed. Like most railwaymen of this period he was given a nickname. These were given to anybody who had something about them that was deemed unusual, be it in body or behaviour. Eddie got his from being thin and consequently narrow across the hips, thus he was 'Snakehips', a label first given him by Running Foreman Jack Tiley. He was part of the team that lobbied in vain at No 10 Downing Street against the closure of Exmouth Junction on 23rd January 1967. Sadly, with closure a forgone conclusion, he began his last turn as a railwayman and remembers with a degree of poignancy how, at 12.00 midnight on the 6th March, 1967, he started his last shift as 'spare' and finished it in tears.

Unless you have been in a job that was your life's ambition, it may seem hard to understand the emotions that could cause a grown man of the 1950s to be so upset. With nowhere else to go, Eddie left the railway and joined Exeter City Transport. He was a conductor for eight years, a job he also came to enjoy and which led to his meeting his future wife. He later became a driver and then a one-man bus operator, combining driving and conductor roles. As always immaculately dressed, Eddie retired in 1994.

Eddie Goff taking part on the abortive march to Downing Street in January 1967 in an attempt to keep the shed open.

Photo: E Goff collection

Every shed had its characters. With some it was part of their makeup, others were conditioned by some event or other or because of where they came from. One who stands out in an affectionate way is **Dave 'Gov' Took**, so called because he always addressed those around him as 'Gov'. When responding to a request, such as, "Can you prep No.34002" he would reply, "Aye, Gov". He originated from Wakefield in Yorkshire where he had previously been a signalman, but it seems that following an incident over Rule 55 (in short, this required the driver of a train stopped at signals to report to the signalbox after being held for three minutes to remind the signalman of his presence), he moved south and joined the footplate grades where he teamed up with fellow Yorkshireman, Gordon 'Jock' Pearcy. Dave was a very pleasant, agreeable and knowledgeable man with a ready smile, all the while holding his short curly pipe to the side of his mouth. He always had a friendly word, though it perhaps took a while to understand his strong Yorkshire accent, especially to those more used to a Devonshire 'burr' - but it was worth the effort. A keen photographer, he would warm to his subject and was quite capable of taking a while to explain some aspect of his hobby. 'Gov' seemed to be skinned in his steam-era uniform with his undersize serge jacket done up by the centre button and his grease top seemingly stuck to his head. I never saw him without it. Unfortunately no one knows what became of him after closure, and Smokey would love to make contact again.

A copy of the engine duty allocation sheet for 1st June 1959.

Courtesy of the Rev. D Hardy

Maintenance Staff

The implementation of the 1955 modernisation program, and its rapid acceleration through the 1960s, resulted in the untimely demise of the steam locomotive, regardless of age, some being only five years old. These locomotives were replaced with untried diesel technology, resulting from one of the worst examples of political interference in the running of the railway. This led in turn to a massive overspend and a tragic waste both of men and machines. Sadly it did not end there and over the years continuing short-sighted cuts, made in the name of economy, continued until privatisation in 1994.

To keep a steam locomotive operational requires a large dedicated work-force, prepared to commit to the work involved regardless of the conditions. That improvements and changes needed to occur was highlighted by the 1955 trials of the five prototype diesel-electric locomotives developed by the LMS and SR companies which entered service from 1947 onwards. These locomotives and their crews, for a time all operating out of Nine Elms (London), covered the Waterloo to Exeter and Waterloo to Bournemouth and Weymouth services, replacing the relatively new Bullied Merchant Navy Pacifics. The trials certainly showed the way ahead but a gradual replacement program, taking several years to allow the technology to improve, made far more sense. The prime example was the then West German (Deutsche Bundesbahn) railway method, in which both electric and diesel traction was introduced over a period of time as technologies improved and became viable. They also did not scrap steam until 1978, a full 10 years after British Rail.

Though the new traction was supposed to be cheaper to run, it was not always the case, certainly in the beginning. The cost of production was ten times that of a steam locomotive (at 1960 prices). Savings in the operating and maintenance of the new locomotives eventually made up the difference between build expenditure, though this took years to get right. The resulting changes also had a human cost and, when one considers the men involved, and the work they did, it is no surprise that many hard-learned skills were condemned to the same fate as the locomotives on which they worked.

The first of the trio of Southern diesel prototypes, No.10201, waits at Exeter Central to return to Exmouth Junction after bringing in a train from Waterloo in the early 1950s.

Above - Left to Right, Nos.80038, 31853, 34002 'Salisbury', 31859 and 41295 on shed on 17th June 1964.

Below - The Grafton 2-ton steam crane used for lifting buckets of clinker and ash when clearing the disposal roads photographed on the same day. *Photos: Mike Jacobs.*

Above - No.41295 being coaled alongside an unidentified member of the 'N' class. The water spray to keep the coal dust down can just be glimpsed above the latter's tender.   Photo: Mike Jacobs.

Below - The old order changeth! Like a cuckoo in the nest, D6313, a Western Region diesel hydraulic type 2 locomotive built by the North British Locomotive Company of Glasgow (later class 22), nestles between two classic Exmouth Junction residents in the form of two unidentified Maunsell S15s. The diesel lasted barely a decade, the steamers four.

Norman Warren, 'Johnny' Watts and Joe Black with the centre wheel set removed from a Merchant Navy pacific.
Photo: Reg Lang collection.

It is to these skilled men and their trades that we now turn, to their life within 'The Shed', often a dark and dirty environment, when working on or under the locomotive or inside the boiler. Even so the camaraderie in the shed was strong and most of the men would always stand by each other, regardless as to whether the problem was personal or work-related; if help was needed it was there to be given. The atmosphere was good because the shed had a strong belief in itself, from the Shed Master to the apprentice, each knew they were good at their job but all were always willing to improve and learn.

Mechanical foremen, Boiler Inspectors and their staff

During the war the foremen worked two shifts, 6am-2pm and 10pm-6am, the time in between being covered by the leading fitter.

Frank Mitchell, 1940-1959 (days); Horace Moore, 1940-1957 (nights); Charlie Smale, 1960-1962; Bob Kiff 1964-1965 (temporary) and Wilson Neal, 1965-1967.

The Mechanical Foreman coordinated the mechanical trades so that work was organised, as near as possible, to enable it to be completed together and on time. Most of this he passed to the Leading Fitter or charge-hand who worked closely with the fitters and workshop, his other duties including daily reports to the District Superintendent and organising locomotives due for shopping (overhaul) at Eastleigh. Because a lot of clerical work was thus created, a designated Shop-man, or clerical assistant, was appointed to assist. The Leading Fitter was the one who carried out the Foreman's wishes and ensured the smooth flow of work while liaising with the Running Foreman when a loco was booked off with a fault but was needed to work a train soon after.

The Mechanical Foreman worked closely with the Boiler Inspector, as well as with the charge-hand boilersmith and his staff. As an example of the coordination between these men, let us consider an S15 that had arrived with leaking tubes and was also due a periodic exam which would entail remetalling and replacing the material (white metal) on the big end bearings of the connecting rods. First the fitters would remove the rods and press out the bushes, the latter

Left - Three 'Bugies' on the jib of the ash crane. Last on the right is Reg Lang. Apart from its obvious use, this crane was used to unload sand from the wagons in the background. Not surprisingly the area where spare sand was stored was known as 'the beach'.

Right - A group of fitting staff on the turntable in 1946. Left to right: Roy King, Johnny Humphries, Charlie Hammond, Gordon Smith, and Brian Joslin
Photo: Reg Lang collection

taken to the workshop for remetalling and machining. Meanwhile the boilersmith and his mate would be working on the tube problem and the fitter and mates would carry on with the rest of the exam. Once completed, the bushes and rods would be reassembled and, with the tubes rectified, the locomotive would be ready for a steam test. When signed off by the Boiler Inspector the locomotive would be ready for service. As the boiler was the most important part of the locomotive, the boiler inspector and his staff had the right to release or stop a locomotive. If there was doubt, they would have the last say.

The fitters were organised into gangs, each having a particular task. The lifting-road gang comprised two shifts, days and nights, their tasks involving work on the running gear, wheels, axle box repairs etc, in fact anything that involved the need to lift the loco. The wheel lathe, situated at the end of the road, was capable of turning the largest wheels, either re-profiling (turning) the tyres to restore them to the correct dimensions or machining the main running journals. If the tyres were worn to a point where it was not possible for them to be re-profiled, then the locomotive would be submitted for work at Eastleigh.

Great care was needed when lifting and packing a loco as only one end could be lifted at a time. When axle boxes needed repair it was normally because of excessive wear on the sides, causing the wheels to 'knock'. For this the wheels were removed and the axle boxes taken apart for re-metalling and machining. When refitting, the sides had to be hand-scraped to get a good bearing fit - too much removed and you

were back to square one, too little and the box would bind causing other problems. Consideration had to be given, in order to get it 'right', to the fact that the frames 'spread' when lifted so measurements were made to calculate the amount of spread and the true size. Getting it right came with experience.

The vacuum gang, or brass gang, largely consisted of older men, with young ones learning the trade. As the name implies their work revolved around the brass components fitted to the locomotive, safety valves, injectors (used for filling the boiler with water), vacuum ejectors (used to create a vacuum for the train brakes), lubricators and clack valves (one-way valves that let water into the boiler from the injectors) etc. Most of this work involved cleaning and repairing the component part, it being rare to fit a complete replacement. Some of this work could be carried out with the engine in steam, although certainly not the case if safety or clack valve work was involved.

X day fitters were quality control men and were a BR introduction. These men checked a locomotive over on a mileage basis and reported any defects found directly to the Foreman. He in turn would liaise with the Leading Fitter who would then issue the necessary work to the Running Gang. These fitters worked a three shift system so that there were always men available for these tasks. They would also carry out any running repairs, booked off by the drivers. Driver's repair cards were first collected by the leading fitter from the Running Foreman, at which point they would discuss the possible effect(s) of the reported defect on the availability of the locomotive. Once this matter was settled, the cards were distributed to the fitters.

Reg 'Flower' Lang on the front No.34044 'Woolacombe' in the early 1950s. Photo: Reg Lang collection

Again, there were many fitters at The Junction, so I can only mention a few of them. **Reg (Flower) Lang** was a local man from a railway family. Always with a twinkle in his eye, he was often looking for the opportunity to pull your leg. A skilled fitter, Reg loved the railway and his work; he was a keen first-aid group member who took part in many team competitions.

As a young fitter in the early 1950s he was sent to cover at Salisbury. Monday to Friday he would sign on at Exeter Central, catch the 7.30am Exeter-Waterloo express, when it was diesel-hauled (often riding in the cab) and return on the 6pm from Waterloo. He might follow this with a twelve hour shift on Sunday in the lifting road at the Junction! This lasted for 18 months.

He was also key member of the breakdown gang and so was often away from home when the crane was needed for bridge replacement work. This might take the gang all over the southern part of the country, even straying as far as the South Midlands. He, along with 'Johnny' Watts, was involved on the lifting road gang where the heaviest work was carried out on locomotives. This took place when engines were separated from their wheels for repairs to the latter, as well as to axle boxes, and inside motion. Such heavy work could be prone to accidents, and it was only the skills of the fitters their mates and the crane driver that kept incidents to minimum. He had been trained, as

No.10201 again, arriving at Exeter Central - 'Flower' may well have been travelling in the cab! The plume of steam is probably from a steam engine in the Exmouth bay rather than from the diesel's train-heating boiler blowing off. These were the Achilles Heel of many early diesels and a true fitter's nightmare

were all the fitters, over a six year period, culminating with a year at Eastleigh. If a fitter was married, wives and children had to learn to endure shift work, difficult with youngsters needing to be kept quiet during the day. In addition when 'on call' the families could be without their men for whole weekends and longer.

During the Winter of 1962/63, Reg, along with others, was away on Dartmoor, working to keep the main line clear of snow, although so severe were the conditions that eventually the ploughs became stuck in snowdrifts, the crews having to find shelter from the wind and driving snow wherever they could. Talking to his wife, Irene, she was philosophical about it, shrugging her shoulders and saying, "You just had to get on with it didn't you".

During this particular time Reg was away for a week, and apart from brief messages sent from the Junction, she did not really know how he was until he came home after being relieved. With only a few days respite he had to turn out again and go back out!

Above - *No.34110 '66 Squadron' on a North Cornwall train at Meldon Quarry on 27th February 1962 is seen from the footplate of N class mogul No.31843.*
Photo: E Crawforth.

Below - *The last duties of the venerable Drummond 'Black Motor' class 700s were as snowplough engines in the bitter Winter of 1962/3. Some members of the class were used after official withdrawal, Nos.30689/97/700 being so used by Exmouth Jct in January 1963.*
Photo: R Lang collection.

Reg got his nickname, 'Flower', from his habit of always calling colleagues 'my flower', a Devonian term used when referring to someone in a Gang. He would refer to apprentices as either 'the buye' or just 'buye' (boy). He still calls me that today, some 45 years later!

One memory I have of him is from the day I started work at the Junction. I was told to report to Reg and Johnny, working underneath a Class 22 North British (NBL) type 2 Diesel Hydraulic locomotive which was having one of the transverse springs on its bogie replaced. As I approached the service pit I heard voices - "Come down ere buye" said one. As I climbed down into the pit, Reg turned to me and said, "Go to the stores and get some Rusties". Not wanting to seem foolish, or fall for some prank (I had been

The 700s were the favoured snowplough engines across the South Western District of the SR and the last remaining members of the class were withdrawn at the end of 1962, a date which saw a holocaust of elderly (and not-so-elderly) locomotives and the transfer of the lines west of Wilton to the Western Region. Exmouth Junction, along with Guildford and Eastleigh, retained some engines into 1963 as they were - literally - indispensible, and in this case, immoveable! The engine with the rather crude canvass shroud is 30697 (the 7 is just visible above the plough) which had been snowed-in near Souton whilst trying to force a way through to Lydford where two more of the class were marooned. N class No.31846 had been sent out four days later to rescue it. The mogul rammed the elderly 'Black Motor' watched by Reg Lang, Albert Davey and the Chief District Motive Power Inspector Sam Smith. Initially its motion was frozen solid, but repeated ramming by the mogul soon freed it up!

The somewhat chilly 'Indian Summer' for these 'Black Motors' only lasted a few weeks as a pair of Q class 0-6-0s was sent to replace them later in January and they were laid up. A year later this engine, No.30697, was steamed to haul No.34067 'Hurricane' back to Eastleigh, the last working of any 700, on 11th January 1964.

All photos: Reg Lang collection.

A young Ray Taylor outside the main entrance to the shed. Photo: Ray Taylor collection.

forewarned!), I made my way to the stores with a deep frown on my forehead. At the store window, the storeman looked at me and smiled: "New here aren't you?" he said. I explained that I had indeed just started and that I had been sent to fetch some 'Rusties'. Expecting a knowing look and some cock and bull story, I waited but, to my relief and surprise, he smiled, left and returned with a bundle of coarse-weave cloths for cleaning purposes. The storeman smiled again at my obvious apprehension and said, "There you are, Rusties". Glad that I had not been had, I returned to the loco.

Bill Batten was another of those men who came from a railway family. He had joined the Southern Railway on 16th July 1942, was interviewed by the then shed master, Mr Steele, and been taken on as a fitters' lad. As soon as he was 16 he started his apprenticeship, learning the trade from the older men, any younger fitters being away at war. He learnt the art of using a hammer and chisel, making gaskets, packing glands, replacing piston and valve rings and the many other tasks necessary to keep a steam locomotive in good repair. Just before his final year as an apprentice he, along with others from the various depots of the Western Section of the Southern Railway, was sent to Eastleigh. Here they became involved with the heavy repair of locomotives, where just about every part was removed and overhauled before reassembly. After the year at Eastleigh he was back working as a junior fitter. In 1948 the new British Railways Southern Region came into being and so began a new era in Bill's career. He enjoyed the work and being a friendly character, he joined in all that was going on at the shed. This often involved the usual practical jokes, frequently using whitewash in some form or another, the main target being the bicycles, on which in those days most men came to work. As a fitter, Bill had to get used to the change in work times and as an apprentice he had worked a 7.30am-5.00pm day. Now he was on a three shift system, 6am-2pm, 2pm-10pm and 10pm-6am, on alternate weeks, including weekends.

During the summers of 1948-49 Bill was sent as holiday relief to the various satellite sheds at Wadebridge, Barnstaple, Okehampton, Yeovil and Templecombe. He preferred Wadebridge which he describes as having been an outstanding place and a good depot. It was during this time that Bill got the nickname 'Basher', quite simply because he had a good eye when using a sledgehammer. He was always accurate when needing to hit something hard and if it needed someone to hold a drift or bar whilst he hit the end, he would simply say, "Don't look at me, keep your eye on the end of the bar". Under such circumstances trust was a necessity so when he hit the bar, you certainly knew it but, as far a I know, he never missed.

Because of wartime commitments, meaning only apprentices and older fitters from about 50 upwards remained on the shed, there was an enormous gap between the two. Due to this, Bill was able to advance rapidly through the ranks to become the youngest Leading Fitter (Chargehand) at just 25. Unfortunately the older men who had declined the responsibility themselves resented Bill's youth meaning he had a hard time when it came to giving orders. During the mid 'fifties Bill as a Leading Fitter, was known for his fairness and did not have favourites to whom others might have given the easier jobs. It helped that physically he was a big man, men seldom argued with him unless there was a genuine difference of opinion.

Like Reg Lang, he was on duty during the infamous winter of 1963 and it was he who had ordered the breakdown crew to man the snowploughs. With the introduction of diesel traction Bill adapted quickly and although his job title did not change, his outlook did, missing the many men made redundant yet accepting that things could not stay the same. On closure and redundancy, Bill readily accepted a transfer to the Road Motor Depot at St Davids, working on the vast fleet of road vehicles then owned and operated by the freight and other departments of the railway. This lasted only a short time before he was offered a job working this time with the Outdoor Machinery (ODM) department, maintaining the plant and machinery associated with track maintenance and other mechanised equipment necessary to keep the trains running. This continued until a change in the whole concept of railway maintenance took place during the1980s and brought about the opportunity to take a supervisor's job, this time as Area Fleet Manager, Exeter, covering the whole of the South West of England. He continued in this role until retiring in 1992.

Today Bill fondly remembers his time at The Junction and can easily recall stories relating to the various characters who worked there. He also takes part in the reunions, proud to have played his part in making The Junction a unique place in which to work.

Next comes a man with an amazing memory, also from a local railway family, whose relatives worked in the area. **Ray Taylor** was a post war apprentice who started at The Junction in 1952 along with a fresh intake of apprentices, all typical of the emerging 1950s culture. They had only known the restraints of war time and now, released from school and being lads together, quickly found their feet and joined in the various pranks and practical jokes then played in a pre-Health and Safety culture. Even so accidents were few, simply because the railway was at the forefront of safety at work, being foremost in the implementation of the Factories Act. With a very good group of first-aiders, who kept their eyes open for potential problems or unnecessary risk-taking that was inevitable in an engineering work place, pranks seldom developed into anything serious. The work was strenuous, as by nature the working parts of a steam locomotive are large and heavy and the men had to operate in often very awkward cramped areas. It was into this environment that Ray and his young colleagues entered, expecting to work hard and also mindful of the older fitters they worked with.

In those days you expected to get a clip round the ear, or worse, if you 'wrong-sided' your elder, but if you were willing to learn, these older men took great pride in passing on their trade and its many variant parts.

Although not every job was pleasant, Ray enjoyed every part of his training and could see the overall picture of where it was taking him. He had no ambition other than to be a good fitter, equal among his peers and ultimately, in a position to share the trade with the next generation of apprentices of which I was to be one. Ray finished his apprenticeship at the main works at Eastleigh, very much enjoying his time there, taking notice of all he was taught and making many long lasting friendships in the process. He regards his time there as one of the best experiences of his working

Inside the frames of a Bullied on the lifting road, temporarily with the centre wheels removed. This shows the 'spoon' big-end looking towards the centre piston and slide bar.   *Photo: Ted Crawforth*

life, witnessing the rebuilding of the first 'Merchant Navy' (No. 35018) in 1955/6. It was during this time that he got engaged to Jean, his wife of over 50 years.

As he was preparing to go back to Exeter for the wedding he asked the foreman if it were possible to leave early in order to get back in good time. The foreman did not give him an answer, so Ray waited till the end of the lunch break and was puzzled as there did not seem to be anyone about. It was not long before everyone seemed to gather around him at once, causing more puzzlement, until he realised that the men had collected together for a wedding present for him and Jean. This sort of thing was not done at the Junction and to this day he remembers with warm affection the men at Eastleigh and their gift.

After a spell of National Service, he rejoined Exmouth Junction and now as a young fitter, went to work with the redoubtable Jim Mares and his team doing Periodical Exams on the as-built Bullied Pacifics. Jim Mares was a hard man to work with, being very particular about the job and expecting those working with him to be the same. There were no fun and games with him - you did the job and did it properly or he would want to know why. Jim was a clean worker and after the exam was completed and the loco back in service, he and his team would clean the pit before starting another exam even though there were labourers about to do it - Jim wanted it done properly. He once said (concerning the completion of a job) "There was nothing nicer than watching a loco after its exam, pulling a train toward Salisbury, climbing up from Central and sounding like a well oiled sewing machine". He developed and made his own tools to enable the job to be carried out more efficiently, and years later delighted in showing them to me.

In those days only basic tools were supplied, anything else had to be made or you made it yourself. The one tool which was universally made, usually by the blacksmith, was the 'pin bar'. One end was pointed and used to remove split pins while the other, flat and chisel like, was used to open up the new pins. The designs varied according to the fitters' needs, as the tool was also used to align holes for brake and valve gear - using your fingers or thumb was asking for

Jim Mares cleaning his Periodical Pit.
Photo: Ray Taylor collection.

trouble and sometimes ended up with a visit to the First Aid room. Ray comments that although Jim was hard to work with, he was nevertheless pleased to have been a part of the Periodical Gang. Being young enough to adapt easily to diesels, with others he was sent to Newton Abbot to be trained on them.

After the clear-out of staff following the demise of steam, Ray was placed in one of four shifts, each comprising four men. There were always two shifts on nights, with one each on days and late turn. The work involved servicing and minor repairs to the Class 42 'Warship' (D800), NBL Class 22 (D6300) and Class 35 'Hymek' (D7000) diesel hydraulics, as well as the class 08 diesel shunters and the various DMUs that covered the local passenger trains. With few spare engines any longer 'on shed' during the day time passed slowly and

Author's pin-bar made by the Exmouth Junction blacksmith.

Rebuilt 'Merchant Navy' class Pacific No.35008 'Orient Line' on the lifting road with wheels and bogie removed the engine supported on packing. The locomotive awaits rewheeling after repairs are completed. The modified locomotives were far more 'fitter-friendly' than the as-built machines, the latter having oil liberally spread around the motion parts and an oil bath that had to be emptied before removal to inspect any part of the complicated chain-driven valve gear, itself rather more difficult to disassemble than the easily accessible outside Walchaerts gear of the rebuilds.

W Philip Connolly/Robert Humm collection

Above - *Exmouth Junction at night in February 1967 - the diesels reign supreme, but not for much longer!*
Photo: R Tacagni

Below - *The Periodical Gang cleaning the pit: no-one was exempt.* Photo: Ray Taylor collection.

the men did not enjoy standing around waiting for work to come in. The night work was very different and they were kept busy when all the machines came in for servicing. Sadly the once-proud depot now showed signs of age and decay, water leaked through the roof and, with it not being fully occupied, it was cold and draughty in Autumn and Winter.

The Machinists and the workshop

The Machinists' duties involved working on the lathes, shapers and vertical millers in the workshop used for all forms of machining. Their workshop was situated just off the end of the lifting road with, at one end, furnaces for the blacksmith and coppersmith. In the far corner of the workshop was a small office, latterly used by the AWS fitters as a workshop. Inside here was a battery charger and spares needed to keep the units working. Like the fitters, each man working had served a full apprenticeship and would have received all round training so that they would be able tackle any job with an understanding of what the component did and which locomotive it came from. They were the same as the fitters in the shed in that they took their work seriously. The wheel lathe was worked by Alf Williams, and the machine when in operation would rumble and grind away as the ancient gears, now worn, sought to mesh with each other. The overhead crane was kept in a clean condition by its driver Sam Galliver, who exercised great skill in operating, needing his full attention to keep the operations safe, always listening for the orders from the fitters below and responding with a light touch on the controls.

Boilersmiths

The Boilersmiths were led by the Boiler Inspector, and Charlie Humphries was just such a man. These men had the power to say whether a locomotive was serviceable or not, hence their position was possibly the most important man under the Shed Master. Like the fitters, all boilersmiths were required to serve a 5-6 year apprenticeship and would similarly finish their training at Eastleigh. Over the years there were many Boilersmiths, but one who stands out was Bob Shewry, in stature a short rotund man, yet he was able to squeeze through the fire-door to gain access to the firebox, on occasions when the loco was still hot! He was also a valued member of the First Aid group. Their main work was carried out after the locomotive was stopped for a wash-out or if it was reported with a serious problem. Two days were usually needed to allow the boiler to cool down sufficiently for a close examination.

With the boiler washed and cooled down, all the covers on the side of the firebox were removed. Then a tube cleaner would clean all the accessible tubes with a specially made brush after which he cleaned the smokebox and fire box of the residue. The Boilersmith was now ready to carry out a detailed examination. He would check the tubes for leaks in the smokebox - this was done by checking for stains around the seams - and whilst he was there he would also check the superheater tubes and elements. If there was a problem with the elements then any work carried out was done by the Fitters.

This was followed by a detailed inspection of the firebox but to do this it was necessary to enter the firebox by going in backwards, no job for someone suffering from claustrophobia The equipment used was a lamp, either electric or more commonly one of the Carbide Acetylene type, and a small hammer. Once inside he would visually check the brick-arch after which it was the tubes, using the hammer to tap

*A pair of repair cards made out during the closing days of steam for ex-LMS Ivatt class 2 2-6-2T No. 41321 **(upper)** and ex GWR Pannier tank No.3759 **(lower)**. Both these engines were allocated to Exmouth Junction in the latter days of steam from their originating Regions.*

the stays and listening for the right response, or 'ring'. A dull sound meant the stay was broken and would need to be replaced. Several hundred stays needed to be checked in this way so depending on the size of the firebox it could take quite a while.

If a boiler tube needed replacing the end was first split using a round nosed chisel and the end then collapsed, this was always done at the fire box end and the old tube drawn out through the smokebox. When refitting a new tube in place, the tube ends were expanded to create a steam tight seal. If a superheater tube was found to be defective and could not be repaired, the locomotive was usually submitted for shopping at Eastleigh where the whole of the smokebox had to be removed to gain the necessary access.

One boilersmith who came to the Junction in the 1950s was Alan Milward who arrived whilst still an apprentice having commenced his work at Stoke-on-Trent together with his father and brother. One of the last was Bill Parry. When steam finished at Exeter, Bill was loaned to Templecombe on the Somerset & Dorset line until that shed too was closed on 5 March 1966. He then returned to Exmouth Junction working with Bob Shewry. Now they maintained the diesel steam-heating boilers - which was quite often (as per Smokey's earlier comment!). Commensurate with redundancy the men had to find alternative work and in some cases new trades. Some would join insurance companies examining heating boilers and other pressure vessels, such as air compressor tanks on an annual basis. I recall one of these coming to check such a tank at the Road Motor Garage where I continued my apprenticeship after the Junction closed. Working with Mr Bulleid's steel fireboxes in the past also meant some of the boilermakers had been required to gain skills in welding, a useful asset following the end of their time on the railway.

Coppersmiths

The coppersmith's job involved not only working with copper in its various forms, mostly pipe-work, but also any small job working with thin plate, such as tin for lamp repairs and sheet metal as used on the casings of the Bullied Pacifics. Terry 'Moon', so called because of his character change with the lunar cycle, was indifferent, but his opposite number, Sid Clifford, was a very skilled man. Thin, he gave the impression that a good rush of wind would blow him over but there was a rod of steel running through him. He did not suffer fools but was always willing to help. Sid Richards was his apprentice and there is no doubt that he would have been well-taught.

Blacksmiths

One must not confuse this job with that of the rural blacksmith for, although the work was basically similar, i.e. working with a hot iron and a forge, in reality it was quite different. The blacksmith was called on to repair any piece of metal that was damaged or broken, repairs being effected by welding, using both gas and electric processes. He was also a toolmaker, making and repairing chisels, pin bars, drifts and any other tool that might be required by the artisan staff. During the war an additional blacksmith was sent down with the fitters from Ashford, each working a two shift system of days and nights. Bert Hobbs was the Junction 'smith with Jack Leaworthy as his striker, joined by 'Treacle' Keen from Ashford and his striker, 'Jumbo' James.

AWS Fitters

AWS fitter was a job that was created with the introduction of the BR Automatic Warning System in the late 1950s and needed a man able to understand electrics as well as being a fitter. George Low was not a railway trained man, coming to The Junction after his time in the RAF during the war. When the SR- and LMS-designed diesel locos came to The Junction in the early 1950s, George was called upon to carry out any repairs simply because he was the only man with any diesel experience. The engines were fitted with Napier turbochargers and any work needed was done only with the driver in attendance. George had been trained by Napier, a nautical engine company that manufactured engines for motor boats and generating sets and he had also served on the RAF rescue boats. In railway history, Napier became famous for the Deltic engines fitted to the English Electric Type 5 locos. George carried on with the AWS work until the end of steam. When the WR AWS fitter, Jack Jordan, came up at the closure of Exeter St. Davids steam shed, he took over following years of experience with the more widely used WR system. George moved onto the new WR diesels until the shed closed.

Fitters and Boilersmith's Mates (Some Fitters' Mates were also trained as Van Drivers)

These men worked alongside the fitters and boilersmiths as pairs resulting in strong bonds being formed, some lasting many years. So close were the working relationships that each knew what was needed from the other often without a word being spoken. Sadly, with the arrival of the diesels, fitters' mates became almost labourers overnight, required only to fill fuel tanks, sand boxes and the engines and transmissions with oil, as requested by the fitter.

There were exceptions where the mate was working with his original fitter and here the team would, where possible, work in unison. One such was **Bob Tacagni**, a man who should have been a fitter in his own right, but joined the railway just too old to start an apprenticeship and so instead became a 'mate'. He did however progress to become a brake-fitter, a job just below a trained fitter. This involved replacing worn brake blocks and adjusting the brakes when required. With the end of steam he reverted back to a fitter's mate, becoming a van driver as well. He was a skilled photographer and some of his photos appear in this book. Such was his ability that in 1965, he was asked by Foreman Wilson Neal to take a series of photos of a damaged Carden shaft removed from a Hymek diesel loco, to be included in the report being made by Wilson to BR headquarters. He was often asked to take photos at staff get-togethers. Jack Warwick and Charlie Franks were also brake-fitters, also with the added duty of van driver and were often required to run errands, delivering messages and picking up stores from Exeter Central or St David's stations. If there was a problem that didn't need the breakdown vans or crane, then the fitters/electricians would be ferried to the incident by van. This happened in 1966 when a Class 35 Hymek failed at Sampford Peverell (now Tiverton Parkway) with a damaged final drive and, over two days, men were ferried to remove the damaged parts and make the locomotive safe to travel to Newton Abbot.

The boilersmiths' mates main duties were much the same as the fitters' mates in that they assisted the boilersmiths with any two-handed job, such as replacing boiler tubes, firebox stays and riveting. Again, men stayed paired for years but they were less fortunate with the ending of steam as their duties were no longer required and all were made redundant.

Norman Warren, 'Johnny' Watts and Joe Back working on the centre wheels removed from a Merchant Navy Pacific. *Photo: J Watts collection*

Other Grades at the Shed

This title covers duties the other grades carried out at The Junction and these were equally important. It was vital that everyone from the Shed Labourer to the Shed Master carried out their duties efficiently for if either one or any in between failed to come up to scratch then everyone ultimately felt it and the shed suffered. Listed below are the remaining grades.

Shed labourers

These men looked after the cleaning of the main shed: this work entailed cleaning the pits after a locomotive had been removed, and involved clearing up the oil and sand spillages. Another area was the mess rooms, this included cleaning the floors and tables as well as keeping the kettles full - these were kept going all the time on the various gas stoves. The workshop had to be kept clear of swarf (metal shavings) and the area kept clear of items that someone might trip up on. The toilets and wash hand basins were important areas that needed their attention and this was done on a daily basis. Keeping 'The Hod' filled with sand and making sure its coal fires were well fed was a job especially favoured during cold weather and often other staff would pop in for a warm as there was no central heating in the main shed. By and large the Labourers were good at their job, though some took more pride than others. The place was never allowed to look overly dirty or neglected, the foremen from the various departments saw to that. One man who stands out is 'Black Bill' Morgan, who was quite a character, a shed labourer who, no-one now knows why, reacted strongly to someone imitating a cow! A loud mooing was sure to wind him up and have him chasing the culprit all over the shed. When confronted he would say "I don't fere you, why you fere me?" (for fere read interfere). This only served to make matters worse and many a prank was played on poor Bill. Some labourers were allocated specific jobs such as cleaning the mess rooms, workshop and offices involving work on keeping the waste paper bins empty, sweeping the floors etc. The worst job they had was cleaning the Drop pits, (see Chapter 5 on Working the Shed).

Firelighters

By the title it's clear that it was their job, when the locomotive was ready for service after repair or washout, to build the fire. They used scrap wood, usually from the scrap bin of the Carriage and Wagon depot across the way, and live coals from 'The Hod'. With the fire burning they had to make sure that the water level was right and the controls correct, regulator closed, cylinder cocks open, reverser in mid gear and handbrake on, so that once steam was raised there was no danger of the locomotive moving away. It took about 4-5 hours for a head of steam to build and, during this time, they had regularly to check the condition of the fire. Their busiest times were Sunday afternoons when the engines had to be made ready for the Monday morning, with some duties starting as early as 01.00hrs.

Boiler Washers

Their job was to clean sludge and other deposits from the boiler after the locomotive had been allowed to cool right down. There was a set time for each class of locomotive to be washed out, usually after intervals of several weeks. To do this all the 'mudhole' doors, oval-shaped, about 7" (17cm) across, on the outside of the firebox, were removed to gain access to the inside, as were the plugs from the back of the boiler, accessed from the footplate. A special copper nozzle was then forced into each hole and connected to a hydrant on the shed floor. This was supplied with water from the high tank behind the shed, the height of which gave enough pressure to clean the boiler effectively. Mr OVS Bullied, the last Chief Mechanical Engineer of the Southern Railway, had adopted the French 'TIA' water treatment system, in which briquettes were placed into the water tanks or tenders of the locomotives to extend

Sam Board steam cleaning No.34038 'Lynton' in 1959.

Photo: W Philip Connolly/Robert Humm collection

the washout period and keep silt and deposits in the boiler to a minimum. After completion of the washout the plugs and doors were refitted and the locomotive was then ready for the boilersmiths to carry out an exam or, if no attention was needed, then the firelighters were free to do their job.

Coalers

At one time this was one of the heaviest and dirtiest jobs on the depot but when the coaling plant was built along with the new depot this all changed. The job of the coaler was to keep the coal hopper full and to efficiently load the tenders and bunkers without spilling or creating too much dust. To load the hopper a wagon was moved on to the tippler table using ropes and electrically driven capstans. Using controls at the bottom, the tippler and wagon were hoisted by a heavy duty Electric motor situated on the top of the hopper. Once the wagon was empty it was lowered and the next one was made ready for the process to begin again. There were two types of chute, one for tank locomotives and the other for tenders. To load a locomotive with coal it was moved into a position with the chute aligned with the tender or bunker, a lever attached to the chute was operated and, using skill and judgement, the right amount of coal was allowed to flow. If the weather, and coal, were very dry, then sprinklers attached to the chute were turned on to dampen the ensuing dust that could rise up from the locomotive. Once completed the locomotive was moved either to the turntable or stabled.

Glandpacker

All steam locomotives have glands, not the same as human glands though! They are situated wherever a part of the locomotive is in direct contact with steam, such as valves and pistons, the regulator, some cab fittings such as blower valve, injector live steam valve and so on. Normally at Exmouth Junction these items came under the jurisdiction of the fitter. However as with things Bullied, the regulator gland was different and needed special attention, so a fitter's mate, Bert Rosevear, a very able man, was given the job and apparently made special tools for the purpose which enabled him to do the job efficiently and quickly. The gland packing was in two halves, so before renewal the old packing had to be removed and this is where the special tools came in; once this was removed the new was fitted, making sure that the ends overlapped so as minimise any chance of steam blowing past.

Water Tester

Without doubt the greatest improvement across the board was the introduction by Bullied of the TIA system, which neutralised the mains water to such an extent that boiler washouts could be lengthened to up to 56 days; this meant locomotives stayed in service longer, thus reducing down time and thereby costs. It seems incredible that no other Region adopted this system. To keep it functioning correctly the water in the tenders and tanks had to be tested regularly and so another job was created, that of water tester and Phil Issacs was the person chosen. It was he who would take samples usually at boiler washouts or, if a loco was stopped for repair or exam, take them to his office and test the water for the correct content. The chemicals came in round Briquettes about 3" across by 3" deep. They were packed in drums and could be readily recognised by being painted a beige colour to distinguish them from oil drums! In most colour photos of Southern sheds these drums can be seen in the background, usually near the water column.

Engine Cleaners and Messengers

Under the steady eye of Charlie "Chopper" Caldicott and George Adamson, the young lads who hoped to be footplatemen first joined as cleaners and were instructed in the art of cleaning. The work was hard and dirty and was carried out using a mixture of paraffin and oil with which they cleaned the whole locomotive. The newest recruit was given the dirtiest job of cleaning below the footplate including the removal of grit and oiled grime from the valve gear and rods. The older one got the sides, boiler, tender and the back of the boiler in the cab. Any brass work was brought to a shine using crushed Bath brick mixed with light oil. The main line locomotives had priority followed by the secondary line ones and then any loco that was spare and needed a clean. These duties lingered on when the diesels came but, with the changes taking place, men wanting to be drivers became 'second men' and didn't do any cleaning. In the days before everyone had a telephone the young cleaners who had bicycles, or latterly motor bikes, were often sent out as messengers to notify Footplatemen of any late changes to the rosters, to cover sickness. They were sometimes used to notify/rouse the breakdown staff in the case of a callout.

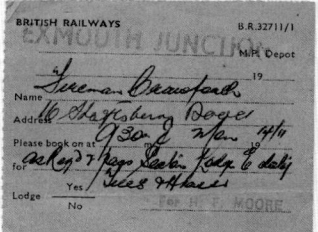 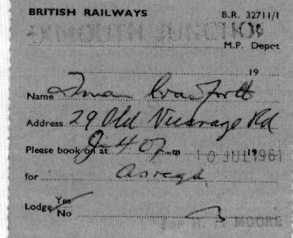

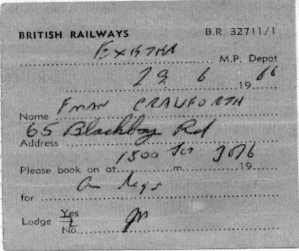

A selection of call-out cards made out to E Crawforth.

Chapter 4
The Breakdown Gang and First Aid Group

The chapters about the Breakdown Gang and the First Aid group have been deliberately grouped to run together as there is a definite link between the two. This connection is one word: 'accident'. The first to do with railway infrastructure and the second to people.

The two were often linked, especially in the event of mishap to a passenger train, where the breakdown gang usually had a couple of first aid men in the make up. Thankfully no serious incident happened during the period being described in the South West. The area covered by Exmouth Junction's breakdown gang was from Yeovil to Okehampton and Bude. However, although the sheds at Yeovil, Barnstaple, Wadebridge and Plymouth Friary were equipped with basic re-railing equipment, for anything serious the Exmouth Junction gang would be called out, hence their potential area was 'all points west of Salisbury'.

The breakdown gang consisted of the Mechanical Foreman, at least two fitters and several fitters' mates, with the charge-hand cleaner undertaking the duties of Guard. The total number called out varied according to the size of the incident.

There were two breakdown trains at Exmouth Junction, the first consisting of two vans converted from time-expired mainline coaches, one acted as a mess-van and the other a tool-van. The latter carried all the tools needed, hydraulic jacks, wood blocks or packing, oxy-acetylene cutting gear and associated equipment needed to lift and reposition a derailed locomotive, carriage or wagon. The mess van was equipped for the men to ride in with a couple of the original passenger compartments retained for this purpose. The rest was given over to a galley arrangement in which a stove was provided together with utensils for boiling water and heating food as well as a cupboard full of tinned food.

The second train consisted of a combined mess and tool van and the Ransome and Rapier 45 ton steam crane, DS1580. This was kept on 24 hour standby with the boiler kept warm by a small fire, so by the time the crew had been assembled and the train signalled off the shed, the crane driver would have boiler pressure rising. Upon arrival at the site of work full operating pressure would then have been reached thereby avoiding any delay in setting to work.

The Exmouth Junction Breakdown Crane No. DS 1580 at Yeoford when rerailing a box van in January 1963, with 'Ironclad', No. DS70010 (SR No.749) in use as a Riding Van for the crew.

All Yeoford photos: Reg Lang collection.

Above - *Exmouth Junction's former Breakdown Van No.DS70016 is seen at Exeter St Davids shortly after the final closure of The Junction. This van had originally been built as one of a series of 'Ironclad' carriages in the early 1920s by the LSWR, numbered 1353 (SR3190). Such was the strength of their construction that many were so converted and lasted well beyond the 1960s as Engineers' stock, this one being preserved on the Mid-Hants Railway (Watercress Line).*

Below - *Roy Davey, Edgar Baker, with foreman George Wheeler and Reg Lang pose for the camera at Yeoford.*

Almost done! The box van is carefully lowered back onto the rails at Yeoford.

In contrast to what was possible in the 1960s when every large depot had a breakdown crane, nowadays there are very few left in the entire country. As an example in the derailment of a an HST set at a Leeds depot in November 2009, it took several hours for cranes to travel from Margam, Wales and Wigan Lancashire to Leeds. In the Paddington crash (October 1999), when a commuter train leaving the station ran past a stop signal and into an incoming HST express, the heavy lifting was done by special road cranes, sourced from outside contractors whilst by the time investigations were finished it was several months before the station was fully open again. Such things were unthinkable forty-five years ago, when getting the line cleared and trains running again was paramount. A classic example was the horrific Harrow and Wealdstone crash, in 1953, when three passenger trains collided in thick fog, causing a terrible loss of life. Yet by the next day trains were running again albeit on a reduced timetable.

Most of the incidents related here and concerning The Junction were relatively minor, such as locomotives or wagons derailed after rough shunting or going through catch points. An example of the distances sometimes covered by the gang can be illustrated by recording the incident that occurred at Holsworthy goods yard on the Bude branch, on 8 August 1964. Here a brake van had run through some catch points and was completely derailed. The crane and vans were dispatched, hauled by No.31845 with Frank Watts and Ted 'Smokey' Crawforth on the footplate. The site was some 50 miles from Exmouth Junction hence travelling to and from plus the actual rerailing occupied all day.

The normal procedure on arrival on site was for the Mechanical Foreman to liaise with the other foremen from the yard/depot, or permanent way department and the signalman. They would assess the situation and come to an agreement as to the correct course of action, such as protection of the area and whether there was a need to remove or switch off telephone/electricity cables. If the latter were deemed necessary the relevant departments were informed and their own men dispatched to the site. Once this was done, the foreman would consult with his staff as to the best way to effect a speedy re-railing. All the men worked as a team, each knowing his place and job. First, packing was unloaded and then the jacks. Safety was uppermost in their minds so the work was steady with no rushing, each piece of packing and the placing of the jacks being carefully thought through. If the crane was being used then it was a case of making sure it was safe, the outriggers carefully packed so as to avoid any fear of the crane toppling when effecting a lift. The placing of the lifting beams and hooks went through the same process, care being taken to avoid further damage to the derailed vehicle.

When a locomotive was involved, weight alone usually necessitated the use of the crane, as illustrated by the photos of the incident in 1956 when Nos.30954 and 34050 met at the neck of Exmouth Junction yard, both trying to get to the same piece of track! The work involved separating the tender from No.34050 to gain a closer position in which to lift this locomotive before moving on to recover No.30954. It may seem as if people are just standing around doing nothing, but in reality the situation is being carefully assessed both before and continually whilst lifting is taking place. In Exmouth Junction yard for instance, there were numerous overhead cables to be considered and also the proximity of the work to the main line with trains still passing nearby: keeping services running was a top priority.

Above - Z class 0-8-0 shunter No.30954 and Pacific No.34050 'Royal Observer Corps' being rerailed in 1956 having blocked access to the shed roads at the critical point! Photo: W Batten coll'n.

Right - Reg Lang and Frank Warren re-railing No.41307 at Exeter Central. Photo: Exeter Express and Echo

The next photo (previous page) is of 41307, derailed outside the carriage sidings at Exeter Central. The engine had jumped the tracks at the neck of the sidings and the entry to the Exmouth bay. This incident caused considerable disruption as both the Exmouth branch line was busy and the carriage sidings constantly in use. Swift action by the breakdown gang meant the area was cleared within a few hours and normal service resumed, before the evening rush hour. Those involved included Bob Kiff (Acting Foreman), Reg Lang, Frank Warren and Sid Wellaway.

With the transfer of the depot to the Western Region and its subsequent run down, the Exmouth Junction crane was moved to Newton Abbot. Not surprisingly this caused some dismay allied to the conviction that the Junction's days were numbered. Soon after this a derailment occurred at Exeter Riverside yard, which had recently been enlarged due to the closure of Newton Abbot's Hackney yard. The crane was called for and, as it approached, one of the Newton crew shouted down to the Junction men "a'ha, we've got your crane" to which Reg Lang's response was, "maybe, but we've got your yard". No more was said!

I remember going on one derailment in 1965 to Exeter St David's station where a parcels van had ridden over the buffer stops in No 2 bay platform. It seemed the only way to get it off was with the breakdown train engine, powered by No.34007 *Wadebridge*, which happened to be the only locomotive on shed laying over until the evening stone train was due. A strong rope was attached to the hapless van and after some slipping by the loco it finally crashed down from its temporary perch. After this we were able to jack it up and traverse it across and back on to the rails. No sooner had that job been completed we were directed to another incident, this time at the gas works - about two miles distant - where a couple of wagons had become derailed. Because No.34007 was too heavy to negotiate the works sidings, we were taken by the station pilot, a diesel shunter. All in all, a good morning's work. As far as I know, this was the last time a steam locomotive was used on a breakdown train in the south west.

The crane wasn't always used on breakdowns. At weekends, the time when most of the civil engineering work on the railway was being carried out, the crane and the gang would be sent wherever the need arose. One such job was the replacement of the old 'bowstring' bridge at Newton Abbot by a new one. In some cases, two cranes would be used, the other coming from another shed. Often the work would take the crane outside the local area and it wasn't unknown to work on other regions - this was because not many sheds had 45 ton capacity cranes, the more common type being the smaller 36 ton variant.

Right - *J Warwick and Reg Lang checking the crane during bridge work.*

Below - *Replacing the old 'bowstring' bridge at Newton Abbot in the 1960s.*

Photos: R Lang collection.

To be a member of the gang involved meant being dedicated to the job. It went beyond just being ready to do overtime as the gang were on continuous call and might be woken up at all hours of night (or day). This was in addition to their regular shed work. Hence all were volunteers.

Thus if, like Reg Lang and John Watts, the working day had just been completed on the lifting road, a call for a breakdown to Okehampton could be very inconvenient. However, such was the commitment of these men that it was never really a problem. When this occurred a message was usually sent to the homes of those involved and they just got on with it, even though they might now not get back till 2 or 3 am in the morning. A clear example of this was during the winter of 1962/63 when the whole country, and Devon in particular, was subjected to intense cold and a large quantity of snow was driven by strong easterly winds into substantial drifts, especially across Dartmoor, the highest point at which the railway operated.

On the night of 29 December 1962, a train became trapped near Lydford and Exmouth Junction was called upon to supply snow ploughs and the men to operate them. As well as the footplate crew, members of the breakdown gang were called upon to join the operation. These men were on call, day and night, for nearly two months, sometimes being away for days on end. A fuller description of those events appears in the book *A Winter Remembered* by the author, and the photos on pages 45 and 46 herein also refer.

The First Aid Group

For many years the railways had encouraged the practice of first aid in all their stations and depots. The groups or teams were supported by the St Johns Ambulance Association who would supply training manuals and support.

There had been an active First Aid group and competition teams at the Junction for many years, this reached a peak during the 1950s when the top 'A' team won the coveted Grand Prior cup, given for a country-wide competition against all other railway teams and St Johns groups: this was quite an achievement. The team that won - with a near perfect score - consisted of Johnnie Almond, Roy Davy, Cecil Lake (Captain) and Bill Carpenter. The 'B' team comprised Jack Tiley, Bob Shrewry, Horace Stratford and Reg Lang. Other men who took part in subsequent teams were Fred King, Ron Moffat, Sid Davey, Jack Aplin, and, latterly, me, Bob Trevelyan. Blacksmith Bert Hobbs was class Secretary, later replaced by coppersmith Sid Clifford. As can be seen in the photo, the 'B' team took the honours on another occasion!

Whilst those mentioned above, and others, did so with some dedication, it must be mentioned that to encourage knowledge of first aid and with it how to render assistance in the event of accident, there were many men who just took the exams because of the benefits that resulted. Each man was given the incentive of an extra day of annual leave and a free travel pass.

Subsequent to winning the 'Grand Prior', the teams continued to do well and were regarded as the ones to beat during the 1950s and 1960s. At this stage those involved included Horace Straford, as Captain, with Jack Aplin, Reg Lang, Fred King and Bob Shewry. The last competitions the teams took part in were held during February 1967. The first of these held at Plymouth, on the 9 February, the 'A' team being beaten into second place but winning the Southern Rose Bowl: they were pipped by their old rivals, the Carriage and Wagon team, who took the Boles Cup.

On 14 February the 'B' team, led by Ron Vince (Captain), with A Parker, R Sene and D Sheldon, took first place, winning the Southern Railway Shield. The semi finals took place at Bristol on 16-17 March, although by this time Exmouth Junction was no more, the depot having closed so it is not known if any of the former depot teams took part. Following this those who had remained on the railway found a place in other teams notably the Exmouth Junction Carriage and Wagon team who quickly became renowned as the ones to beat.

Mrs C Williams, wife of the District Traffic Superintendent Exeter, presenting the cup for gaining first place in the District 8 (Group 2) British Railways ambulance competition, held at the Liberal Hall, Yeovil, to Jack Aplin, captain of the Exmouth Junction Loco 'B' team. With him are Jack Tiley and Reg Lang, amongst others. (Undated but believed to be late 1950s).

Chapter 5
Exmouth Engines and Working the Shed

The allocation of engines to Exmouth Junction had, up to the rebuilding of the depot, been made up from a motley collection of old 19th century with some new early 20th century locomotives by Robert Urie and Richard Maunsell added between the Wars. This situation continued until the retirement of Maunsell.

With the coming of OVS Bullied, Maunsell's replacement, just before the Second World War a whole new way of thinking concerning locomotive design and construction was entered into. Bullied carried out a review of all the existing steam stock and immediately saw the need to bring it into the middle of the 20th century and to incorporate as much of the modern technology then in vogue into new designs as soon as possible. The first was logical: since the Southern did not have many good quality goods locomotives, Bullied's first design proper was just such a locomotive, the Q1. Quite possibly the most powerful 0-6-0 ever built, it did everything required of it. No embellishments here, just a rugged purposeful machine - it should be noted Bullied was not into aesthetics! The staff used to refer to it as the 'ugly duckling'. The Q1's were never allocated to The Junction, but there are photos which show the occasional one did make an appearance, on goods or engineers trains from the Southampton area.

During the war the next new design to be introduced was also meant to be useful rather than pleasing to the eye, especially when compared with its contemporaries. In a departure from previous wheel arrangements, Bullied went for the Pacific (4-6-2) in an effort to spread the axle loading to meet the civil engineer's requirements. Being the first of its kind on the Southern it broke with all previous Southern thinking. It was clear to see that Bullied was introducing ideas gained whilst working under Nigel Gresley of the London & North Eastern Railway (LNER), but the running gear, the boiler and use of casings around the boiler were pure Bullied. This was meant to be a 'fine wrist watch' compared to the 'alarm clocks' that had gone before - the concept was originally meant to cut down service times and keep the locomotives out there working! However the 'best laid plans of mice and men' came into force and the class ended up needing more specialist care than the locomotives they replaced causing true engineers and some drivers to love them and those that enjoyed the traditional way, to hate them.

So the first of Bullied's 'Merchant Navy's' came on stream. The boiler was an outstanding success with its all welded construction, although the internal enclosed chain valve gear left a lot to be desired. Many books have been written about the Pacifics and Bullied, so it's up to the reader who may want to know more, to read them as it's not the author's intention to put his head into that Lion's mouth! The introduction of the Merchant Navies, caused the replacement of The Junction's long standing 4-6-0 'King Arthur's' and the smaller Pacifics, the 'West Country' and 'Battle of Britain' classes, replaced the L11, S11 and K10 4-4-0s.

With Nationalisation and the formation of British Railways (BR) all future locomotives were to be designed by RA Riddles the new Locomotive Engineer for BR. The next major change in The Junction's allocation came during the early 1950s with the first members of the new BR Standard Class 3 tanks, which were replaced in 1962 by their larger sisters, the Class 4 2-6-4 tanks. At the same time as the Class 3s arrived, and in an effort to replace the oldest of the M7s and the even older O2s, new BR-built ex-LMS Ivatt designed Class 2 tanks arrived and were to stay until the end. With the appearance of the modern locomotives, and the older Adams and Drummond classes being replaced, this left in 1960 just a few retained for specific duties, the most famous of which were the three Adams Radial tanks (4-4-2T) retained because of the severe curves on the Lyme Regis branch. Once the curves had been re-laid and eased the Ivatt tanks took over their duties.

Next to go were the Drummond T9s mostly kept for the Plymouth and North Cornwall lines. The completion of Phase 1 of the East Kent electrification programme in 1959 released more modern classes, so that by 1961 the last of the T9s had left The Junction. It has been said by a former engineman that when they left, the "heart" of The Junction left too. The last of the Drummond classes to remain was the M7 0-4-4 tank: The Junction was reluctant to let these go but the new Western masters prevailed and the last one left in 1963.

The banking duties had, for a long time (since 1927), been the domain of the Maunsell rebuilds of the 1874 Stroudley E1 0-6-0 tank, the E1/R, 'R' meaning the addition of an extra pair of wheels or Radial truck to allow the coal bunker to be enlarged so becoming an 0-6-2T. The last three were at Exmouth Junction. Replacement came during 1960 with all 8 of the 'Z' class 0-8-0 tanks being allocated here. There had been one, 30954, here since the war, used for shunting the marshalling yard at the Junction, but their tenure on banking turns was to last only 2 years.

The Allocation

Since its opening the allocation had been large and made up of a motley collection of old and new locomotives; by Nationalisation and the coming of the Bullied Pacifics things began to change and by closure there were no ex-SR locos left and those that did remain were between 5 and 10 years old. I show below three lists, the first for January 1947, the second, just after amalgamation with the WR in January 1963 showing the final Southern allocation and the third just before closure to steam in June 1965.

January 1947

Local passenger 1897-1911 Drummond 0-4-4T M7 class 24, 30, 34, 37, 39, 46, 49, 55, 105, 124, 133, 245, 252, 253, 256, 320, 323, 356, 374, 375, 376, 377, 668, 669, 671 — Total 27

Local passenger and light goods 1889-1895 Adams 0-4-4T O2 class 192, 193, 199, 207, 224, 230, 232 — Total 7

Banking duties 1874-1883 0-6-2T E1/R class 2124, 2135, 2695, 2697 — Total 4

Lyme Regis branch 1883-1885 Adams 4-4-2T 0415 class 3125, 3488, 3520 — Total 3

Yard Shunter 1929 Maunsell Z class 0-8-0T 954 — Total 1

Light Goods 1883-1886 Adams 0395 class 0-6-0 3029 — Total 1

Mixed Traffic 1901-1902 Drummond K10 class 4-4-0 135, 137, 138, 329 — Total 4

Mixed Traffic 1903-1907 Drummond L11 class 4-4-0 156, 408, 409, 411, 436, 439 — Total 6

Passenger 1899-1901 Drummond T9 4-4-0 282, 283, 301, 722, 723, 724, 725, 730 — Total 8

Mixed Traffic 1917-1932 Maunsell N 2-6-0 1407, 1408, 1409, 1828, 1831, 1832, 1833, 1834, 1835, 1836, 1837, 1838, 1839, 1840, 1841, 1842, 1845, 1847, 1853, 1855, 1856, 1869, 1871, 1875 — Total 23

Goods/Mixed traffic 1927-1936 Maunsell S15 4-6-0 823, 824, 825, 826, 827, 844, 845, 846, 847 — Total 9

Express Passenger 1941 Bullied MN 4-6-2 21C1, 21C2, 21C3, 21C4, 21C5 — Total 5

Mixed traffic 1945-1949 Bullied WC 4-6-2 21C101, 21C102, 21C103, 21C104, 21C105, 21C106, 21C107, 21C108, 21C109, 21C110, 21C111, 21C112, 21C113, 21C114, 21C115, 21C116, 21C117, 21C118, 21C119, 21C120, 21C141, 21C142, 21C143, 21C144, 21C145, 21C146, 21C147 — Total 27

Grand Total 125

January 1963

By now BR had added 30,000 to the original SR ones. It will be noticed that the allocation now included BR tanks as well as a large number of former LMSR Tanks, otherwise the rest were still former SR types, though the addition of a WR pannier tank was evidence of the changes to come.

Yard/Station Pilot WR 1933 0-6-0PT 3679 — Total 1

Passenger 1897-1911 Drummond 0-4-4T 30025, 30045, 30048, 30125, 30667 — Total 5

Goods/Snow Plough 1938 Maunsell Q 0-6-0 30530, 30531 — Total 2

Goods/Banking 1932/35 Maunsell W 2-6-4T 31911, 31912, 31913, 31914, 31915, 31916, 31917, 31924 — Total 8

Goods/Mixed Traffic 1927-1936 Maunsell S15 4-6-0 30841, 30842, 30843, 30844, 30845, 30846 — Total 6

Mixed Traffic 1917-1932 Maunsell N 2-6-0 31406, 31818, 31834, 31835, 31836, 31837, 31838, 31839, 31840, 31841, 31843, 31844, 31845, 31846, 31847, 31848, 31849, 31853, 31855, 31856, 31860, 31874, 31875 — Total 24

Mixed Traffic 1945-1949 Bullied WC/BB 34002, 34011, 34015, 34020, 34023, 34024, 34030, 34032, 34033, 34035, 34036, 34056, 34058, 34060, 34062, 34063, 34065, 34066, 34067, 34069, 34070, 34072, 34074, 34075, 34076, 34078, 34079, 34080, 34081, 34083, 34084, 34086, 34096, 34106, 34107, 34108, 34109, 34110 — Total 37

Express Passenger 1941 Bullied MN 35003, 35009, 35010, 35013, 35022, 35025, 35026 — Total 7

Mixed Traffic 1946 Ivatt (ex LMSR) 2-6-2T 41238, 41270, 41272, 41284, 41292, 41299, 41306, 41307, 41308, 41309, 41318, 41320, 41321, 41322, 41333 — Total 15

Passenger 1952 Riddles BR 2-6-4T class 4MT 80035, 80036, 80037, 80038, 80039, 80040, 80041, 80042, 80043, 80059, 80064, 80067 — Total 12

Grand Total 125

The Zs, although comparatively young, were in need of major boiler replacement so they were withdrawn en masse and their replacements were the larger W class 2-6-4 tanks, displaced from London, a case of a 'hammer to crack a walnut'. They were more than capable for the task and could have stayed longer, but with '1963 and all that' they left, to be replaced by the Panniers. When needed any available tank could be used to bank and often was.

Of the remainder of the allocation all were long standing useful classes, the most notable being the Maunsell 1917-design N class 2-6-0. So versatile were they that they were never truly replaced as their duties largely disappeared with them in 1964; what duties did remain were covered by the BR class 4 4-6-0s and the 2-6-4 tanks. The heavy freight traffic was covered in the main by the Urie/Maunsell S15s, like the Ns also versatile and more than capable of the tasks set before them. They were replaced in 1963 by the BR Standard class 5s displaced from the Midlands and North East England.

It is interesting to note that with all the locomotives based at Exmouth Junction, every footplateman and every fitter-boilersmith had preferred locomotives to work on and this often caused great debate in the various mess rooms. I can recall hot discussions between fitters on the merits of the Bullieds versus the products of Drummond and Maunsell, with one fitter declaring that there hadn't been an improvement since Drummond! There's no doubt that the products of Bullied created the strongest feelings with comments going to and fro especially concerning those rebuilt by BR against the Originals. It cannot be denied that the Originals were freer running than the Rebuilds this being due to the increase in reciprocating parts, 3 sets of Walchaerts valve gear, as opposed to the internal, or infernal, chain drives (depending on your preference!). One can understand the dislike of the fitters getting covered in oil and crawling through the confined spaces of the underneath and the inside of the smokebox, with all its dirt, to gain access to the middle cylinder. Yet those who loved the engineering of Bullied enjoyed the work. The BR Standards were seen by and large as an improvement on what had gone before, pre-Bullied, with their ease of maintenance and disposal, highlighted by rocking grates and self cleaning smokeboxes. With the addition of easy access to all moving parts from outside the locomotive and underneath work restricted to mostly brake adjustments, one can understand why.

Any engineman will tell you that having sufficient space to work in the cab was a prerequisite and certainly the Southern tank locomotives had this. In 1963 at the Western Region takeover when the WR management tried to replace the trusted Southern M7 tank locos and auto-fitted stock with their own auto coaches and suitably fitted panniers, with their smaller cabs, it was greeted with disdain. What made matters worse was the fact that most of these replacement locomotives were worn out, and because of this an Ivatt Class 2 tank was often utilised instead, operating conventionally by running round the train. This continued until the introduction of Diesel Multiple Units (DMUs) on all the East Devon branches in November 1963. By 1965 there was a shortage of DMUs, so two 14xx 0-4-2 tanks, 1442 and 1450, were transferred from Yeovil. Their cabs were even smaller, so again the Ivatts were 'borrowed'. This situation was short lived as more DMU's became available. With the closure to steam in 1965, there were no locos of Southern Railway origin left, the remaining ones being the Ivatts and BR Standards - all between 5 and 10 years old - and the three ex-GWR Pannier tanks kept primarily for banking.

Three lists have been compiled, the first for January 1947, a year before Nationalisation, the second, just after take over by the WR in January 1963 and showing the final Southern allocation and the third just before closure to steam in June 1965. Looking through the Allocation lists and coupled with the workings the locomotives were allotted, one is able to build a clearer picture of why certain locomotives were based at The Junction and why some stayed long after their sell-by date. I have started at the beginning of the BR era as this is the general scope of the book and to make it a bit clearer I have shown the main working for each class, followed by its build date and designer.

June 1965

The final allocation was kept solely for Banking, spare duties and freight and was readily replaced by class 22 and 35 diesel hydraulics.

Light Passenger 1932 Collett 0-4-2T 1442, 1450 — Total 2

Mixed Traffic/Snow Plough 1930 Collett 0-6-0 2214, 3205 — Total 2

Banking/Station Pilot 1930 Collett 0-6-PT 4655, 4666, 4694 — Total 3

Mixed Traffic 1946 Ivatt (ex LMSR) 2-6-2T 41206, 41216, 41223, 41249, 41291, 41307, 41308, 41321 — Total 8

Mixed Traffic 1951 Riddles BR 4-6-0 4MT 75008, 75022, 75025 — Total 3

Passenger 1951 Riddles BR 2-6-4T class 4MT 80035, 80037, 80041, 80064 — Total 4

Passenger 1951 Riddles BR 2-6-2T class 3MT 82030, 82039, 82040, 82042, 82044 — Total 5

Grand Total 26

Exeter Central station was *the* place to see locomotives allocated to, or visiting, Exmouth Junction right up until the end of steam on the West of England main line. Here almost all trains stopped to exchange engines, remove bankers or be remarshalled for their ongoing journeys. The station was a 'frontier' between the main line from London and the group of lines in Devon and Cornwall known as the 'Withered Arm', due to its shape when viewed on a map.

Through the years the locomotive types varied but the need for a station pilot, or pilots, and bankers was always crucial and these engines were often 'off shed' for much longer times than those used on some main line turns.

Above - M7 No.30044 is seen on station pilot duties on 20th August 1959. *Photo: Bill Wright*

Right - BR Standard class 3 2-6-2T No.82025, usually to be seen on Exmouth branch trains, stands in the Up platform alongside Z class No.30952, normally seen banking trains from St David's, on the same day. *Photo: Bill Wright*

Below - Salisbury's long-standing resident 'Merchant Navy', No.35006 'Peninsular & Oriental S.N. Co.', waits for the road back to the shed on the down through road after bringing in an express from the east on 25th July 1959, just 11 days before entering Eastleigh Works for rebuilding. *RCTS CH00250.*

Above - Maurice Dart recorded No.34079 '141 Squadron' on the down end of Exeter Central's up through road on 7th April 1963. The engine was a 72A (83D) locomotive from 24th February 1958 until 14th September 1964 when it went to Eastleigh, surviving there until 27th February 1966.

Below - Maurice was at Central again to photograph Salisbury's visiting Rebuilt No.34089 '602 Squadron' on 5th September 1964. On the **left** it's seen awaiting the road to the shed and on the **right** passing the 'dummy' which gave it authority to head for The Junction. Maurice well remembers the driver walking past it with a vital teacan!

Disposing a loco coming on shed.

It is customary when recording an account of a visit to a locomotive depot for the writer to start from the entrance and continue with the walk around: in other words as the shed appears to a visitor on foot. Instead I will describe it from the locomotive crew's perspective: from coming on shed and going through the various processes involved in disposing and stabling - at Exmouth Junction of course! In this chapter I have used, with permission, some notes from 'Smokey' - these are shown in italics.

"The shed was arrived at from the main line via a series of crossovers and double slips leading to the throat of the complex. A double slip, with the road automatically set for the ash pits, was first approached. If the locomotive was due to go straight to shed then the point was open to allow this, but if not then the way led to one of the two ash pits. The arriving crew would hand over to the disposal men and then proceed to book off and write up any faults that they had discovered. The disposal men, usually a driver and fireman rostered for this, would then set about their duties.

"When you disposed an engine (as a fireman), you joined it on the drop pit and immediately got up on the tender or tank to fill from the water column; meanwhile the driver was examining the engine for any possible defects. Whilst the water was being replenished it was back to the cab to turn on the blower and the injector, the latter to fill the boiler. Then find a three-quarter inch spanner, shovel and brush and clean the smokebox. Invariably ash and char would have been dropped on to the front framing so this had to be swept away. Then it was back to the cab, get out the clinker shovel (or slice), dart and pricker to clean the fire. You cleaned from side to side.

"On BR Standard types with their drop grates the fire was pushed forward and clinker dropped into the ash pan from the back half, then you would pull the fire back and drop the front half in a similar manner. While doing this, it was your job as fireman to check the condition of the tube plate, brick arch and firebars (the driver might lend a hand with the fire if he wished). Usually you would put an engine on shed with a little fire left in the box, made up right under the door. If the loco was to be set aside for further duty then the remaining fire was left in but, if not, the whole was removed. Next it was underneath to made sure the ashpan was clear. By now the water tank would be full, so it was out with the pipe from the column and proceed to take coal.

A view of the ash pits. Ash and clinker are prominent in the foreground and the drop pits are to be seen between the rails on both roads with the water tank and columns ahead of them and the coaling tower prominent in view.

Two views of 'Battle of Britain' No.34069 'Hawkinge' being disposed over the ashpits. Clearing out the smokebox, full of hot ash, with the residual heat coming from the boiler, was a hot and filthy task.

'Hawkinge' was an Exmouth Junction locomotive from 19th March 1954 until the Western sent it packing back to Eastleigh for scrap on 23rd November 1963, by which time the Southern had no further use for it. It was one of only four Light Pacifics to go to its grave with an unmodified tender, all four being engines taken over by the Western Region on 1st January 1963.

Photos: Amyas Crump collection.

Above- Maunsell S15 4-6-0 No.30825 on the ash road between a Light Pacific and the ash crane on 22nd December 1963 seems to be in need of maintenance work as the right hand cylinder cover is missing.

All heavy maintenance was done in the 'Cathedral' so this engine must have had work started on it but was then 'dumped' outside as the S15s were being withdrawn by this time..

The engine had just lost its handsome flat-sided Maunsell tender and received this flared-top one from a withdrawn Urie S15, but, despite the massive load of coal, it was all to no avail as it wasn't repaired and was condemned the following month and sent to Barry in South Wales to be scrapped. However, it wasn't and today works on the North Yorkshire Moors Railway.   Photo: Maurice Dart.

Below - In happier times (20th August 1959) the ash crane is seen behind M7 No.30021, resident at Exmouth Junction from March 1951 until it was reallocated to Salisbury in September 1961.

Above - *No.34002 'Salisbury' being turned on the 70' turntable installed in 1947 to accommodate the Bulleid Pacifics. On this occasion, 17th June 1964, the vacuum assistance seems to have failed!*
Photo: Mike Jacobs.

Right - *Very near to the end of steam at Exmouth Junction, Western Region Standard class 4 4-6-0 No.75025 stands outside the shed in a very woebegone condition. The Western didn't just treat the ex-Southern engines shabbily, they allowed their own engines to deteriorate in their quest to be the first BR region to eliminate steam, the plan being to finish a little over a year after this Maurice Dart photo was taken on 6th December 1964. No.41307 is behind No.75025. The identity of the Original Bulleid Pacific to the right is unknown.*

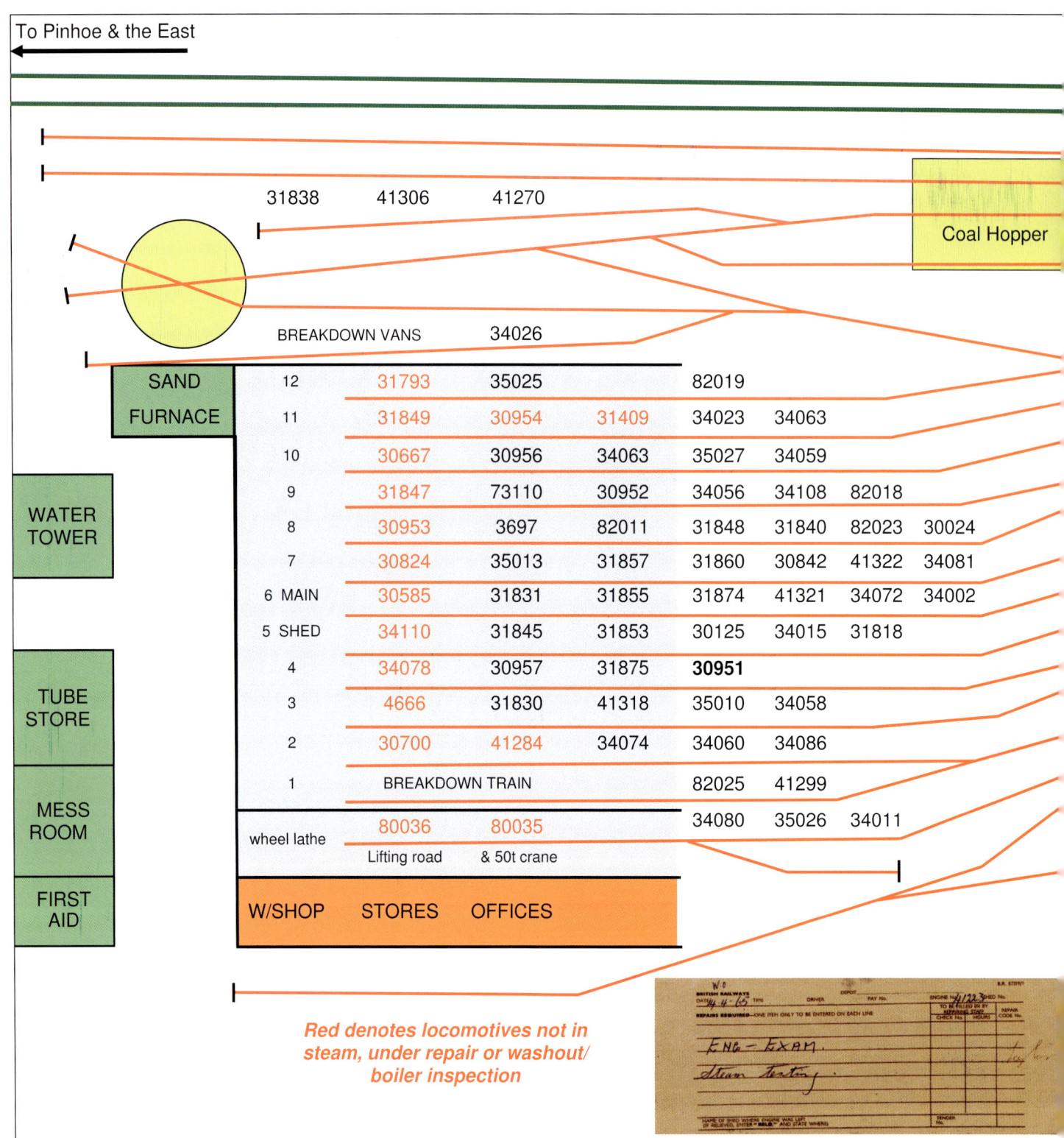

"With the locomotive coaled and watered, the next move for a tender locomotive was to the 70' turntable which was vacuum-operated. This meant that when the loco was on the table the vacuum brake hose was connected to a longer one fitted to the table's vacuum motor, the vacuum coming from the locomotive's main ejector. This in turn powered the motor to turn the table, via a gearbox. Windlass-type handles were provided as a back-up for manual operation should the motor fail or when it was necessary to turn a dead locomotive. Once the locomotive was turned, the shed turner was then consulted. He would check his shed list **(see table above)** which gave him the required position in which the locomotive was to be placed, this depended on

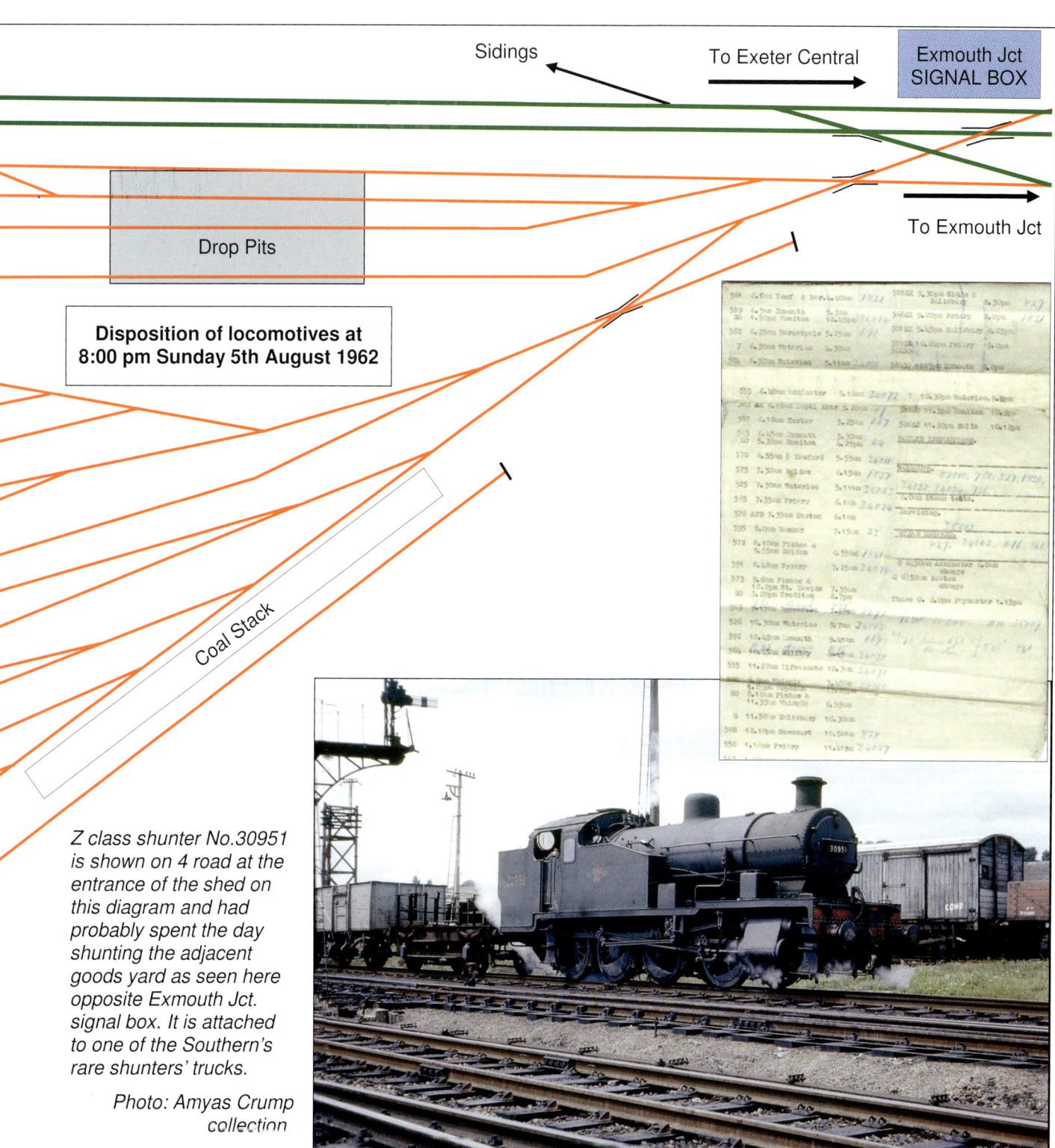

Z class shunter No.30951 is shown on 4 road at the entrance of the shed on this diagram and had probably spent the day shunting the adjacent goods yard as seen here opposite Exmouth Jct. signal box. It is attached to one of the Southern's rare shunters' trucks.

Photo: Amyas Crump collection

whether it was for repair/service or stabled ready for its next rostered duty. In accordance with this requirement the locomotive was placed on the most suitable shed road. A lot of planning went into this since too many locomotives in the wrong position not only meant a lot of work for the shed staff but could lead to delays, especially on summer Saturdays.

Once stabled, It would be left for the firelighters to keep their eye on it. Occasionally you might strike lucky and get a soft number which meant that someone had already done the fire and all you had to do was coaling and turning. With the locomotive stabled the disposal crew walked back to the arrival roads for the next locomotive to be dealt with".

Above - On 20th August 1959 Nos.34023/34079/34110 stand outside the shed ready to take trains to Plymouth, North Cornwall and North Devon as the Summer Saturdays season reaches its zenith.

Right - A Standard class 4 tank, No.34030 'Watersmeet' and No.35010 'Blue Star' warm up on the roads as they await their turns on 7th April 1963.
Photo: Maurice Dart.

Although not part of the shed layout, nor under its control, Exmouth Junction signal box nevertheless played an important part in the smooth running of the shed, for without an alert signalman movements to and from the shed could have been severely disrupted. It was the pointsman's duty at the shed entrance/exit to alert the box regarding locomotives leaving the shed and good coordination thus resulted in prompt departures and arrivals. During the summer months, especially Saturdays, Exmouth Junction signal box was kept very busy controlling movements on the main line, the Exmouth branch, the goods yard and the loco shed. Not surprisingly it was manned 24hrs a day.

"When preparing an engine, you as fireman would climb aboard and as a first automatic reaction give the handbrake a tug to ensure that it was on. Then check the water level in the boiler and look at the state of the fire. Engine oil, thick, and paraffin cans were then collected and taken to the stores for filling. The fireman then filled a feeder (oil can) for the driver, who had started his own examination and oil round. You filled the sandboxes, tightened the smokebox door, trimmed and filled the lamps, lit them if needed and checked the tools: bucket, brush, spanners, fire irons, coal pick, shovel, gauge glass replacements, detonators, red flags, disc boards etc.

"If the engine was due to go out shortly, the fire was made up, but if not the fire was left and the driver would likewise leave the trimmings out. Otherwise when a crew came on later who might be booked for final preparation, they would make up the fire and top up the coal/water before departure. Sometimes engines were made fully ready without a set duty in case it was wanted by the foreman as a spare".

Right - *One of Ivatt's class 2 2-6-2 tanks (affectionately known as 'Mickey Mouse' tanks) is seen inside the Lifting Shop or 'Cathedral' in the gloom at the back end. The hook from the overhead gantry crane is poised to perhaps lift it to enable the fitters to attend to some normally inaccessible parts.*

Its general condition indicates this must be something minor as major faults tended to result in withdrawal at this late date, 11th April 1965.
   Photo: Maurice Dart.

Below - *Another of the big Z class tanks, used for shunting or banking duties, is seen behind a Rebuilt Pacific on No.2 road whilst an import from the Western brings a reintroduction of the BR class 3 tanks after the Southern allocation had gone some 5 years earlier.*
   Photo: Amyas Crump coll'n.

Above - 'Merchant Navies' were for two decades the principal express locomotives of the Southern, Exmouth Junction having at least five of the class on its books for most of that time. They handled all the principal express trains on the West of England main line to London Waterloo, most notably the ACE or 'Atlantic Coast Express' which was composed of through carriages to virtually every terminus in Devon and Cornwall served by the Southern. No.35012 raises steam on 22nd December 1963 in another classic Maurice Dart view.

What is perhaps less well known is that they also handled goods trains at night, thus justifying their designer's claim that they were true 'mixed traffic' engines.

Left - The 'order of battle'. Well, perhaps not, since we have no views of 'Battle of Britains' on these pages: this is a form showing duties of locomotives for a summer day in the 1950s. Two local 'specials' have no booked engines!

Beauty and the beast. **Above -** *After its adventures in the snow at the turn of the year the 'class leader' (it wasn't actually the first built) of Drummond's 'Black Motors' was consigned to store by the time Maurice Dart photographed it on 7th April 1963. Of course, we all have our own interpretation of that old saying, but No.34003 'Plymouth'* **(below)** *was making a good attempt to take the more complimentary of those titles whilst blowing off steam on one of the shed dispersal roads.*

This time it's 'little and large'. **Above -** *The Southern never built any large passenger tank engines after the disaster to one of its 'River' class 2-6-4 tanks at Sevenoaks in 1928, so the Drummond M7 tanks carried on until nearly the end. No.30024 is seen alongside the shed in the company of one of its T9 contemporaries, No.30719.*
Photo: Amyas Crump collection.

*The large Maunsell Z tanks were favourites of photographers around Exeter: there were only 8 of them in total and this is No.30951, posed **(below)** outside the Carriage and Wagon repair shops that were adjacent to Exmouth Junction shed whilst 'in store' on 7th April 1963.*
Photo: Maurice Dart.

Chapter 6
The Meldon Ballast

This is a previously unpublished article written by Ted 'Smokey' Crawforth in 1981, recalling his days working from Exmouth Junction shed on the heaviest regular goods trains of the Southern, the legendary 'Meldon Ballast'.

Because the general public does not, on the Southern Region anyway, usually travel by goods train, the enthusiasts and the press tend to give rather too little attention to what has always been much the more important part of railway business. South West England, although the birthplace of the world's mining industry, is not associated with heavy freight or mineral haulage, but when I was firing at Exmouth Junction we handled a fair amount of traffic, mostly general goods moving in and out of the region. Among our regular jobs were the express services such as the famous 'Tavy' goods, which we took between Exeter and Salisbury. We also worked the ballast trains from Meldon Quarry, just outside Okehampton.

The LSWR began extracting granite from Meldon in 1897, since when it has supplied several hundreds of thousands of tons of ballast for the whole Southern system. The resulting hole in the ground is huge and will probably remain to puzzle many future generations. It lies on the edge of Dartmoor, near the 950 feet summit of the Plymouth main line, adjoining Meldon Viaduct, whose steel lattice towers can still be seen from the A30 about two miles outside Okehampton. The ballast was carried in vacuum-fitted hopper wagons of 40 tons capacity. A typical load would be ten of these and a brake van, grossing about 600 tons. From Meldon to Exeter the road is all down hill (similar to the better publicised descents from Shap or Beattock) except for two short stretches at North Tawton and Bow, so a 2-6-0 (N Class) was quite adequate to handle the train down to Cowley Bridge Junction, where we always got stopped before being allowed to venture on to the Western. Sometimes a 'West Country' might be used, or on one occasion we worked ten loaded hoppers down with a LM2 41xxx tank! As we virtually coasted over the 25 miles or so, there was naturally a tendency to try and see how far one could run. Consequently, speed varied from a walking pace to 60mph, indeed I remember with an N class and ten on, one of our younger guards got out of his van as we came up to the summit at Bow, and pretended to push!

Whilst this was going on, Okehampton would phone Exeter to advise them the weight of the train and the motive power on it so that the right banking engines were available. That little LM2 tank would have required three engines, one on the front and two on the rear, but on most occasions with an N, S15 or WC they had just two behind. The bankers could be any type, 700, an N or a WC, but mostly the designated bankers, initially the E1R's and, when these were replaced in 1959, the Z's and in 1962 the W's: by the end of steam it was ex-GWR Pannier tanks. I believe the train was generally over-powered rather than under, because there were two or three sets of catch points on the bank, used to prevent trains running back down the bank, and we couldn't undergo the humiliation of having the stone train stuck and trying to get that little lot on the move on a sharply curved and 1 in 37 graded bank. There weren't many sound recordists about in those days, but there were cameras recording it, and it certainly was a sight to see, especially at night, pounding up the gradient amid all that smoke, steam and glory!

Maunsell class S15 4-6-0 No.30846, the same engine as the one in the text, but here seen during the day, moves off shed for its next duty on 20th August 1959.
Photo: Bill Wright.

Meldon Quarry Staff Halt and the small engine shed which housed the Engineers' Department shunter. USA class No.DS234 had replaced the last G6 tank, No.DS682, a few weeks before this snow-clearance train swept past and over Meldon Viaduct on its way to Lydford on 30th December 1962.
Photo: Ray Lang collection.

Left - *LMS Ivatt tank No.41315 pauses at Meldon Quarry Halt for the workmen returning home after a day's work.*   Photo: E Crawforth

Opposite - *In the final years of steam, following the Western Region takeover, up trains from Exeter St. David's to Exeter Central would be banked by that Region's own Pannier tanks, heavy freights such as the Meldon ballast workings necessitating at least two of them. Seen here is a general freight with a Standard class 4 tank at the head end and a few ballast wagons bringing up the rear.*
Photo: Amyas Crump coll'n

The booked timings for the 9.25pm Okehampton to Woking stone train that we worked to Templecombe, and the return empties from Wilton to Exmouth Junction were:

TIMINGS FOR MELDON BALLAST TRAIN WORKING

	Outward		Return		Out Miles	Return Miles
Okehampton	dep	9.25 pm			00	
Coleford Junction	pass	10.02			14	
Crediton	pass	10.10			18	
Cowley Bridge Junction	arr	10.24			24 ¾	
	Dep	10.31				
Exeter St. Davids	arr	10.35			25	
	dep	10.38				
Exeter Central	arr	10.43			25 ¾	
(Start of "Smokey's" run)	dep	12.20 am			00	
Exmouth Junction	pass	12.25	arr	6.30 am	01	84 ½
Sidmouth Junction	pass	12.50	dep	5.41	12	73 ½
			arr	5.40		
Axminster	pass	1.30			27	58 ½
Chard Junction	pass	4.51			53 ½	
Yeovil Junction	pass	2.20	dep	4.10	49	36 ½
			arr	3.33		
Templecombe	arr	2.50	dep	3.05	59 ½	26
(End of 'Smokey's' run)						
	dep	3.12	arr	3.00		
Wilton South	pass	4.13	dep	2.10	85 ½	00
Salisbury	arr	4.20				

Now, dear reader, please imagine yourself transported in time and space to Exmouth Junction Motive Power Depot. Today is Friday, 9th March 1962, and it is half-past ten at night. We are due to book on at 10.55pm, Driver Frank Churchill and me, Fireman 'Smokey' Crawforth; our engine is S15 No.30846. After signing on and reading the notices, I go out to join the engine: she stands in the dim light of the shed yard floodlights, waiting for me to climb up on the footplate. After tripping over some lumps of coal left by the firelighter, I hang my bag on the hook in the cabside - there are boxes on the tender for your gear, but they are always messy with oil and coal dust. Dig out a duck lamp from the box under the seat, light up and we can survey the situation.

A fitter's duck lamp from Exmouth Junction, a similar one would be used by the footplate staff.
Author's collection

The first thing you look at whenever you board a steam locomotive is, of course, that the handbrake is on, then the boiler water level. We have a full glass, 60-100lbs on the 'clock' (pressure gauge) and the fire is up under the door. There is a fair amount of soot around the boiler back: remember this 1962, not 1982, there aren't sixteen blokes polishing one engine, and since '846 is a goods engine she probably hasn't seen much cleaning recently. Not to worry, I crack the blower off the face to clear the smoke, collect the engine oil bottle, cylinder oil bottle and paraffin can, and go off to the stores for oil.

Returning with the oil, I fill a 'feeder' (oil can) for the Driver and stand it on the tray above the firehole door, along with the bottles by the boiler back to warm up.

Now to fill the hydrostatic cylinder lubricator; checking that it is turned off, I drain the water off (the drain cock is operated by tapping with a ¾ inch spanner), remove the filler plug, top up with cylinder oil, replace the plug, turn the lubricator on.

I next check the tools: three lamps, bucket, brush, shovel, coal pick, three fire-irons, two discs, detonators, red flags, gauge glass, spanners and (most importantly) the tea can. With the three lamps lit I get off the footplate with them, the brush and the ¾" spanner - the latter is the fireman's right hand. This time it is used to check the smoke box door lugs, and the brush is to sweep down the running plate on both sides.

Two lamps go on the tender to show the headcode for going down to Exeter Central and I always take one with a red shade and put it on the middle bracket on the engine as a taillamp. The drill is that when you get to Central you can take the other lamps off, put one up on the footplate, take the other one round and put it on the smoke box. The third one you only have to turn to white; then if anything should happen en-route and you have to go round the front of the train, you know where you can immediately and safely put your hand on a lamp with a red shade in it. Being properly organised in this way means avoiding the hesitation and delay which can sometimes create accidents.

While we're out there, I look in the sand boxes - we're in luck, someone on 'tools and sands' duty has already filled them. By now Frank has arrived at the engine, and I tell him that the oil is ready. Frank is a quiet type, but he is quite cheerful as he puts his bag on the driving seat, looks around to see what he's got to work tonight, then begins his examination and oiling. While he does that, I go to work on the fire, open the back damper a shade and push down the fire that's there, which may cover, say, three-quarters of the grate. We need some good lumps as a foundation to build on, so up on the tender to fetch some down. Then make the fire up: how much? Well, as much as it needs; experience of doing the job every day in all kinds of conditions will teach you the right amount.

Now we are ready to move, first to the water column to top up the tender; we test the injectors and sands, then leave the fireman's injector on to top up the boiler. The 'pet-pipe' works off it, so I can wash down the cab and boiler back, and dampen the coal. When the tender is full, but not overflowing, I make sure to put the lid on and check that the coal is trimmed down safely. Back in the cab I shut off the boiler water gauges and clean the gauge glass protectors in a bucket of hot soapy water in which I also wash my hands. Then the final job, yes, you've guessed it - make the tea!

It is now 11.55pm and we are due off shed; we have a look out both sides, a touch on the whistle, and we creep down the yard to pause near the pointsman's hut. The pointsman has a clock in his office and usually looks out to see us moving slowly down. One of us will call down: "light engine to Central for the 12.20 stone". He then phones the signalman and gives us the tip when the "dummy" (ground signal) comes off, and we're away tender first to Central.

As we run down to Central station we see from the signal indication on the gantry that the train is in the up goods yard tonight. The guard is with the train, after having a look round it and is standing at the front ready to beckon us on to it. While he is giving Frank the details

Later still, the Western used some of the dreadful NB Type 2 diesel-hydraulics as bankers, often together with a steam engine as they couldn't be relied upon to get to the top of the bank safely! D6336 'helps' a Meldon Ballast working up the 1 in 37 gradient over Bonhay Road and into St. David's Tunnel in 1965.

of the train, its weight, speed limits etc, I couple up including the vacuum pipe as this train is all piped; as soon as I sing out "all together!" Frank opens up the small jet vacuum ejector to check that he gets 21" on his brake gauge in the cab. I change the lamps around, then back on the footplate to find that the guard has scrounged a cup of tea. After that he goes back to carry out a brake test, while I check the fire's right before leaving.

The need to have the fire right when working a heavy train should be clear if you look at the gradient profile of the route and do some simple arithmetic. If you place our 600 ton train on a 1:100 gradient such as lies between us and Exmouth Junction, there is a force of 600 tons trying to pull us back down the slope, which is getting on for half the rated tractive effort of the engine, itself only a theoretical figure, so the fireman has to be on top of the job. After that first climb we can run down to Broad Clyst, but we then face thirteen miles, eleven of them uphill at around 1 in 100, to Honiton summit. After the steep descent to Seaton Junction, comes the twelve mile climb up the Axe valley to Hewish, then the road is what the books call 'undulating' to Templecombe and beyond. I can expect to be firing at regular intervals at least as far as Yeovil Junction and perhaps up to Milborne Port, shovelling a couple of tons of coal. Frank will be driving by his experience and the feel of the weight of the train behind, with the 'cut off' (similar to changing gear on a car) anywhere between, say, 35 and 50%, not that it matters because no-one can see the scale in the dark anyway.

Meanwhile at Central the signalman has got the road right for us, so as soon as we see a green lamp from the Guard's van we are ready to go. Frank sets her at about 65% and gently moves forward to take up the slack in the couplings (not all the wagons are screw coupled). Exchange signals with the Guard, just to make sure he coming too! Now she's straight into the bank at 1 in 100, with the fire doors shut and damper three-quarters open, and Frank's three-quarters regulator will brighten that fire up a treat on the section up to Exmouth Junction. In the meantime I am looking out to spot the double arm signal at St James Park and then through Mount Pleasant tunnel and on to catch the wave from the signalman at Exmouth Junction signal box. Frank now eases the regulator back and winds her up to 35% cut-off as she runs onto the down gradient. I turn my injector on, then the next signal I am watching for is Pinhoe distant, and I indicate to Frank that it is 'off', or clear. Off goes the injector after passing Pinhoe box; Frank has opened her up again, so I start firing two down the front of the box, two to the middle, two at the back, producing

Smokey (Ted) in the cab on 10th May 1962.

as much steam as is needed, but not too much: that's boiler control. I look out again to catch Broad Clyst signals, now we are into steady climbing past Cranaford Gates level crossing and on to Wimple. Apart from the signal indications, Frank and I don't have much to say to each other; we are both getting on with our jobs. Most of the time just a raising of the hand gives Frank the information that a signal he is expecting me to see is 'off'. The vital signal to look out for is of course the distant signal, at this time of night some of the signal boxes will be closed for the night, whilst others are still in operation, and the next one to look out for is Sidmouth Junction. As we pass the empty station, the box appears as a square of light in the darkness, just a silhouette in which the signalman seems to float by with a friendly wave to indicate that everything's all right and we are doing well. "Better than it was last week" comments Frank, with a wry smile - on that trip we had reached Sidmouth Junction when a big lump of coal jammed in the tender front and I broke the shovel in trying to get it shifted. We fired the rest of the way to Templecombe using the remains of the shovel and a spare disc board!

From Sidmouth Junction she dips her nose down the descent at 1 in 100 to Fenny Bridges (an ancient crossing point on the River Otter and the site of a battle in 1549, for those of you that like these details). Here we go over four bridges in quick succession. Then it's more steady climbing, through a dimly lit Honiton station and on up to the entrance of the three-quarters mile long Honiton tunnel. About a quarter of the way through the tunnel the gradient changes in our favour, so as the train comes over the summit, Frank eases the regulator back and finally shuts it, and as he does so I turn on the blower to stop any blowbacks from the downdraft in the confined space of the tunnel. We can now have a sweep up and pour out a cup of tea while the train runs freely down the bank, past Incline Box, where old "Smudger" Smith will probably be sat in his armchair waiting for us to go by. Looking back to the tunnel I watch out to check the Guard is still with us in accordance with Rule 126: the four 'Catherine wheels' at the back end show that he is screwing his brake on, holding the train out tight on the run downhill like a good Guard should.

We hope that he doesn't end up in the situation they had a fortnight ago when there was some paraffin spilt on the floor of the brakevan and in the run down the back the Guard managed to set the van on fire with the sparks from the wheels! This was spotted by the signalman at Incline Box, who alerted Seaton Junction, where they stopped the train and put him out. He said "it was the Indians, shooting flaming arrows!"

As you come towards Seaton Junction looking for the distant signal, you will see it cross from one side of the engine to the other in the spectacle glass before you go underneath it. We pass the signal box, and another Signalman floats by in the dark with a wave. We feel the Guard release his brake as we run through the station and under the bridge, on down through the bottom of the

A daytime view of the climb to Honiton incline summit from the cab of Standard class 5 No.73044 on 28th February 1964.

Both photos: E Crawforth

The fireman's view, taken from the cab off No.34078 on 22nd August 1963 as No.34107 passes. Photo: E Crawforth

dip by Whitford Village, alongside the River Axe, which we cross seven times before reaching Chard Junction. The next signal we will be looking for is the 40' high Axminster distant; now Frank is picking her up on the regulator again, and by the time we get to Axminster he has it a good three-quarters open, the rest is over and I'm firing again, putting a round into the box at regular intervals. There are two crossing gates on this section, at Wadbrook and Broom, but they are usually locked out.

The next box is Chard Junction, it's over on Frank's side so he'll get the friendly wave. Whenever possible I will walk across myself, to double-check the signals, have a look at the box we are passing, and generally satisfy myself that everything is in order. Then back to firing, for she's still working up the long bank to Howish, passing the crossing (where I am told there were sidings during the war) and over the top at mile post 133 ¼, and Frank eases her back as we go down through the tunnel to Crewkerne. "Here, how many cups of tea have you had? I've seen you have four, I've had five and the can's still half full!" questions Frank - it turns out the regulator gland has been leaking into it.

On down through Crewkerne station, the Guard starts to wind on his brake a bit to keep the train tight till we get down to Hardington Bottom, another place where sidings were put in during the war. Here we pass over what we used to call the "silent mile", the first section of continuous welded rail on the Southern Region (I believe that when the line was singled in 1967 it was taken up and used somewhere on the Western). I feel the brake come off and away we go again, up the hill to Sutton Bingham where there is another signal box on the fireman's side, and around the corner Frank shuts off steam just after the box and we run down through Yeovil Junction, past Wyke Gates which are also locked out at night, on as far as Sherborne distant. In later years the box at Wyke Gates finished up in the crossing keeper's back garden.

We pick up them up again and pass Sherborne's distant, this is one we can both see as it is on a slight curve, then up through Sherborne itself and on to a steep bank, a couple miles at 1 in 80 to Milborne Port. Then we get over the final summit and down into Templcombe and a gentle easing into the station aiming to stop her right for the water column.

The stone train stands in the station simmering in the quiet night, the injector is singing as we fill the boiler to keep her quiet and avoid disturbing the local inhabitants. We stand on the up main line as the next up train, the

3.40am local goods from Yeovil Junction, does not arrive until 4.10. By the time we have taken water and washed up the church clock, just over the other side of the S & D line, is striking three and we settle down to wait for the Salisbury blokes to come in with our down empties. We walk over the footbridge and down the platform where the empties have just come in to change over with them and then set off back home.

The timetable shows a long wait at Yeovil Junction, during which time the famous 1.10am Newspaper train arrived, the station staff did their job, and she was off again. If we were running late there was no need to stop there, but if we got caught up by the 5.32am Yeovil Junction to Exeter parcels we would sometimes have to stop at Sidmouth Junction and set back into the down sidings to let it pass. More often than not, though, by 6.30 I would already be on my way home.

So that's working the Meldon stone train in 1962; and what is there to connect us with 1982? Well, that lovely church clock is still there at Templecombe, over beyond where the S & D line used to run, and I still think of those trips when I'm putting in the runner beans. I use that broken shovel handle as a dibber, to this day (2010).

How the Southern did it! In the late 1940s M7 No.30374 pilots 'West Country' No.34041 'Wilton' up the fearsome bank from Exeter St. David's across Bonhay Road and into St. David's Tunnel. Neither locomotive shows any sign of ownership, which dates this to mid or late 1948 or early 1949. The M7 has been outshopped in the full lined-out mixed traffic black livery of British Railways and the 'Spamcan' is in Bulleid's triple-yellow lined Malachite Green.

The train consists of the standard 10 ballast hoppers used to carry Meldon Stone to all parts of the Southern system and there is at least one and, more likely, two banking engines at the rear, again - probably - E1R tanks.

Chapter 7
The End - Rundown and Closure

The single most devastating blow to come to The Junction was the transfer of all lines west of Salisbury (actually from Semley, west of Salisbury), from the Southern Region to the Western Region on 1st January 1963.

Overnight lines and services were under threat as company and later regional rivalry that had existed since the 19th century was now well and truly over and the Western Region had won!

Neither did it take long for the WR to make its intentions known, for within months changes were afoot. This started just three months later with the withdrawal or transfer of the 'W' class 2-6-4T banking engines and their replacement by WR 8750 class pannier tanks. The M7 pull-push engines working the Seaton branch were also substituted by WR pannier tanks of the 6400 class. Later in September of the same year for the start of the winter timetable the S15s had gone, replaced by BR Standard class 5s. Meanwhile diesels, of the D6300 and D7000 classes, made odd appearances, mostly on workings from Plymouth but also for crew training.

In late 1963 the Lyme Regis, Seaton, Sidmouth and Exmouth branch lines went over to DMU operation, but due to a shortage of diesel units steam returned briefly to the Lyme Regis and Seaton branches in early 1965. However this was short lived and as soon as DMUs became available, steam was replaced. Ironically the branches themselves would not last much longer either.

Also, in October 1963, Exeter St Davids steam shed closed and the remaining staff and locomotives, by now mainly diesel shunters, were transferred to The Junction. Up until this time Exmouth Junction had retained its former Southern Region identity as 72A, but this now changed during October, becoming instead 83D (the old Plymouth Laira code), coming under the control of Newton Abbot (83A). At the stroke of a pen Exmouth Junction had been relegated to no more than a running shed.

A night to remember: Ted (Smokey) and Maurice Bevan with No.41320 on the last steam train to Lyme Regis, 2nd November 1963. The cracks were beginning to appear.   *Photo: E Crawforth*

As can be imagined this was no good for the men's morale, already staff were being let go and the rest knew that the proverbial Sword of Damocles was poised waiting to fall.

There was a respite from changes during the early part of 1964, steam still reigning supreme on the main line - but it was a swansong as major changes took place leading up to and beginning with the forthcoming Winter timetable. Major repairs on steam ceased at the end of May, one of the last engines to receive such work being No.73030, which arrived for axle box work. Soon afterwards diesel hydraulic locomotives of the D800 'Warship' class arrived for crew training, the intention being for these to replace the 'Merchant Navy' class on the Waterloo services.

In the event it was only partially successful, for on several occasions the diesels failed and the steam types were called on to replace them. But as major work on steam was no longer being carried out, these once fine locomotives too began to fail and in consequence a mixture of other locomotives, in effect anything that was available, took over the work. Finally it was announced that, as from the September and the commencement of the Winter timetable, the old order of services was to change for good with all main line trains diesel hauled as a two hourly service to and from Waterloo starting and ending at Exeter St Davids. There would be no more through trains to North Cornwall or North Devon and only one to and from Plymouth - the through Brighton service. All other trains would be reduced to DMU operation, although this was quickly found to be insufficient and some of the North Devon services were supplemented with diesel locomotives and coaches. In addition local freight services were withdrawn and yards closed, except for block trains such as fertiliser or coal. Even so not all steam working actually finished, for through to October several former SR locomotives of the N class continued on residual North Devon freight work, that is until the Divisional Headquarters got to hear of it. An enforcement order was immediately put out and the practice was stopped, potential customers and traffic were ignored and steam permanently withdrawn.

With reduced traffic there was a drastic reduction in the locomotive allocation at the Junction, all the ex-SR locomotives either withdrawn or transferred away. What work remained was handled by a few BR standard types brought in mostly from depots that were being dieselised. Indeed for many months the down sidings became a holding place for line upon line of withdrawn locomotives awaiting the call to the breakers yard; one of them, No.34096, had only had a major rebuild just three years previously and was to all intents and purposes just 3 years old.

One in the eye for the new Masters! N class 2-6-0s Nos.31837 and 31846 had been withdrawn in September 1964 but are seen with at least two other members of the class on the ash pits on the day after they dropped their fires for the last time, on 23rd October 1964. Photo: E Crawforth.

For a short while the Lyme and Seaton branches reverted back to steam during early 1965, but this was short lived and as soon as DMU's became available they were displaced. The effect on the men was devastating. The ranks of the enginemen and maintenance staff were severely depleted and consequently the depot no longer rang out with the sound of steam and happy voices, instead it was half empty and almost mute. Now the only time the covered roads were full was at night when the DMUs came in for servicing. Not surprisingly with this came an air of depression, the remaining men knowing worse was to come. They were not convinced that as late as January 1964 assurances had been given that the depot would become an essential part of diesel servicing in the area, to which aim it was officially renamed the 'Exeter Running and Maintenance Depot' though old habits die hard and amongst railwayman SR and WR alike it was still referred to as 'The Junction'.

Yet for all the supposed promises of a long future the workforce were suspicious of the WR management and so they quietly watched and waited to see what would happen. Some relief came with the installation of diesel fuelling points, fitters being trained in the new traction, whilst instead of boilersmiths and the trades of the steam era, even a new skill was needed with a few electricians added to the staff.

June of 1965 witnessed the last engines of the steam allocation withdrawn or transferred, so now the depot was officially closed to steam although it would still see the occasional engine arrive for coal and water having worked from Salisbury. Such engines did not linger.

Any steam drivers and firemen left faced redundancy, the engines they had once worked on withdrawn and awaiting the call to the scrapyards. Ironically these were Nos.41321, 4666, 4694 and 4655, none of which were former SR types, the latter having already departed.

*Western takeover: **Left,** "the only time the covered roads were full was at night when the DMUs came in for servicing" and the D800 diesel hydraulics had taken over the Waterloo services.   Photo: Bob Tacagni*

Below - *The last working steam locomotives to remain on site were ex-GWR examples, the little class 14xx type having been called in to work services on some of the East Devon branches when DMU availability fell. No.1442, seen with 'Smokey' alongside, was to go to Tiverton for preservation. 22nd October 1965.   Photo: E Crawforth.*

Above - Fit only for scrap? A line-up of withdrawn Southern engines on 6th September 1964 includes No.34096 'Trevone' which had been expensively rebuilt in April 1961: it was effectively just 3½ years old and had worked a mere 211,046 miles in this form.
Photo: E Crawforth

Right - A notable visitor on 27th March 1966 was Gresley A4 Pacific No. 60024 'Kingfisher', which was serviced at The Junction whilst working an LCGB 'A4 Commemorative Tour', some way off its usual haunts in Scotland.
Photo: R Holland

Five former GWR types set aside for preservation similarly remained on site, including Nos.1442, 1450 and 3205, but these departed in September. The last two, also destined for preservation, Nos.6412 and 6430, departed in October.

What was left was a demoralised and ageing staff. BR practice had been to dismiss the youngest men first, in the belief they could adapt to new trades more easily than the oldest. However, in some cases it was those closer to retirement who chose to leave, so giving the younger men more of a chance. This was particularly so amongst former footplatemen.

After the shock of 1965 things appeared to settle down and for around 12 months there was little change. Indeed there was some hope for optimism with new cleaners and two apprentices taken on. October 1966 changed all that. News came that the lines from Okehampton to North Cornwall were being closed as were the Lyme Regis and Seaton branches, plus many of the intermediate stations between Exeter and Salisbury. This further reduced the work for all concerned, but worse was to come. During the opening months of 1967, rumours became fact when it was announced that the Sidmouth Junction to Sidmouth, and Tipton St Johns to Exmouth branches were to close whilst worse of all was that the former mainline from Salisbury to Exeter was to be reduced to a single track, the latter especially having the effect of reducing the services between Exeter and Waterloo. Most devastating of all was that 'The Junction' was to close completely, from 7th March 1967.

The men tried to fight and protests were mounted, culminating in a march on 10 Downing Street (in company with the then Exeter MP Gwyneth Dunwoody). Here a petition was handed in but decisions had been made and whilst all were treated with courtesy none of the protests had any effect. The WR steam depot at Exeter St. Davids underwent track rationalisation and was prepared for reopening as a fuelling point for the remaining DMUs and locomotives. The maintenance staff was reduced to six fitters, three fitters mates and three electricians, all others either taking redundancy or transfer to Newton Abbot or the Road Motor Depot. Now the former St. Davids station booking office became the signing on point for the remaining footplate staff. So ended forty years of occupation of the Exmouth Junction site by the Locomotive Department.

Right - *The Men of The Junction go to Downing Street in their bid to keep their cherished Exmouth Junction alive and functioning.*
Photo: E Goff

Below and overleaf - *Sometimes known as a 'Cenotaph' type of coal tower, the concrete structure is stripped bare of recyclable metalwork (below) and then unceremoniously destroyed in October 1970 (overleaf). It would not stand as a memorial to its hard-working and loyal workforce.*

Visits made after closure

On the morning of Monday 7 March 1967, I was taken up to the Junction to collect some of my remaining belongings. The area was deserted as we drove into the depot and parked. Walking through the entrance I was struck by the utter emptiness of the interior of the shed, the twelve roads all quiet, the only evidence of occupation some little piles of sand where eight hours before a locomotive had had its sands checked and cleared. Now the end had come, there were no more calls from the drivers and fireman, no shouted orders from the running foreman and no comments from the fitters to the stores: all had gone. The last man had left at 6am that morning, the final shift going home. We walked, Dick Roach the Storeman from the Road Motor Dept and I, toward the store to pick up bits and pieces. I left him there and went to the workshop to collect the last of my personal effects from my old tool cupboard before leaving it forever. At the time I had not been allowed to take things with me to the Road Motors where I now worked, having been told that there was not enough room. I had felt cheated as I did not believe them. After a final farewell we left, and I remember feeling very sad as this chapter of my life drew to a close although I was determined to make the most of the next stage of my railway career.

A few weeks later I had occasion to go back with Bill Batten to change some axle suspension pads on a track maintenance machine using the lifting road crane. Again the emptiness struck me as memories flooded back, but it was good to return and to use the crane. Across the tracks, on 12 road, the carriage and wagon department staff, who were using it to repair the coal hopper wagons, worked quietly as if in reverence to the old depot. By mid afternoon we were finished and left the depot to its slow decay. My next visit was to photograph the trackless site before final demolition in 1969 and my very last was to witness the demolition of the buildings and coal hopper in 1970.

Postscript

In the May of 1967 I was told that a group of men were going to Meldon Quarry to prepare the last steam locomotive this side of Salisbury, a USA class shunter No.DS234 (formerly No.30062) for its final trip to Cashmores of Newport, South Wales for scrapping. I immediately approached those in authority for permission to join the group, and, after a bit of thoughtful posing, permission was granted. So I joined the last men from Exmouth Junction to work on the last steam locomotive in BR service in Devon. The group consisted of Foreman Wilson Neal, Fitters Johnnie Watts and Ray Taylor with Van Driver/Fitter's Mate Charlie Franks taking us there; it took most of the day to go there, do what we had to do, and come back. We had fun, but it was a poignant time: after this Wilson and Ray went to Newton Abbot, Johnnie began working for Western Fuels and Charlie moved to the ODM and I returned to the Road Motors to finish my apprenticeship.

Appendix 1

Staff known to have worked at Exmouth Junction (1940 – 1967).

Many of these names will have been already mentioned in the main text in context with the roles they fulfilled, however for reference sake the complete lists are provided for clarity. They have been supplied by those who worked there and are listed below; this cannot be a complete list as there is always bound to be someone left out. The list starts at 1940, but many who worked before this date and subsequently carried on into the BR period are included.

District Motive power Superintendent (BR)

Mr A W Johnson

Shed Masters (1940-1967)

Mr E Hoare
Mr R D Steel
Mr Sam Webster
Mr E S Beavor
Mr H Moore
Mr C Smale

Locomotive Inspectors

Sam Smith
Charlie Rooke
Edgar Snow

Running Foremen, approximate order

Alf Yelland
Fred 'Brocky' Brock
Jack Tiley
Jack Tilley
Jack Stevens
Ralf Bartlett
Jeff Priddy 'Mustafa'
Bert Bufton
Ray Down
Henry Turner
Albert Watts

Maintenance staff, approximate order

Mechanical Foremen,

Frank Mitchell, 1940-1959 (days),
Sam Hardy,
Horace Moore, 1940-1957 (nights, then until 1960 days),
Charlie Smale, 1960-1962
Bob Kiff, 1964-1965 (temporary)
Wilson Neal,1965-67.

Leading Fitters (Chargehands)

Reg Palmer, Jack Salter, Jack Vosper, Claud Dare, Bill Babbage, Bill Batten, Bob Kiff, Sid Hollier (ex-WR).

Examining Fitters – Tom Savage, Assist. Bill 'Duke of Cornwall' Jefferies (Days), Arthur Phillips, Asst. Bill Stanbury, Bert Wright, Joe Eden.

Machine Shop staff

Coppersmiths – Sid Clifford, App. Sid Richards.

Tinsmiths – Ted 'Tapper' Phillips, Tom Jury.

Blacksmiths – Jack Vanstone, Striker - 'Bunny' Rabbitts, Bert Hobbs, Striker - Jack Leaworthy, Ted Phillips, Ern Fey, George Leaworthy.

Machinists (Shapers, Drills and Millers) – Sid Stoneman, Cecil Lake, Mike King.

Turners – 'Ginger' Bill Atkinson, Johnny Almond, Bill Lasky.

Shop Officeman – Stan Horne, Tom Babbage, John Ware, Cliff Sprague.

Fitters - Bill 'Chippie' Carpenter, Assist. Norman Archer, Clifford Phelps, Assist. Bill Stanbury, Frank Salter,(Periodical C/H) Assist. Fred Taylor, Then Jim
'Nasser' Mares became C/H, Assist. Jock Finlay, Jim Burwood, A 'Nobby' Clark (Bullied lubricators), Tom 'Wiggy' Wigmore, Assist. Bob Tacagni, Bert 'Acker' Steer, Assist. Big George, Mike 'Oswald' Mullarkey, Assist. Edgar Bauer, Brake Fitter Bert Weare, Assist Reg Langdon, Jack Millward (clack boxes and water gauge frames, WC/BBs and
Standards), Assist. J Woods, Jackie Bauer, Assist. 'Big' Jack Perry, Colin Heath, Assist. Fred 'Piccalo Pete' Bealey, Fred Denning, Ernie Hunt, Charlie 'Dixie' Hammond, Assist. 'Taffy' Penwarden, George Croft, Nat Clifford,
Gordon Smith. Sid Pearcy, George Low, Tom Savage, Fred Punchard, Jim Burwood, George Croft, Basil Ames, Roy Hodgson, Bernard Bidgood, Peter Guthrie, Bert Trivit, Les Pym (ex-WR), Mike 'Ginger' Discombe Fittter (ex-WR)
Walt Reeves (Steam Crane fitter only worked 7.30 – 5.00pm)

Fitters' Assistants often referred to as "Fitters Mates"

Jim Woods (Crane fitter's Assistant)
Tom Babbage, Jock Ditchburn, Henry Quick, Jim Woods
Harold Smith (also van driver)
Len Hill (both came up from the Concrete works on closure in 1963)
George Wheeler, Fred Taylor (Uncle of Ray Taylor), Frank Warren, Sid Wellaway, George Esworthy (Gland packer), Bert Thorne, Reg Cudmore, Charlie Franks, Roy Davey, Joe Back, Jack Rawlings, Lofty Crammer, Taffy Penwarden, Peter Adams, Bert Lilley, George Wheeler, Jack Warwick, Wally Lyons, Joe Back, Jack Finch, Charlie Horn, Bert Lilley, Fred Riley.

'Vac' gang - Leading Fitter Bill Babbage, George Low, Glyn Prothers and App.

Breakdown Steam Crane Fitter Walt Reeves Asst. Jim Woods

AWS/ATC Fitter/Electrician Jack Jordan (WR)

Exmouth Junction Trained Apprentices, Fitters unless stated, approximate order, 1939-1967

Derek Mitchell, Ernest Hunt, Gordon S (Sid) Parker,
Gordon W (Bill) Batten, Bert (Acker) Steer, John Humphries,
Doc Chatfield (wont to war before completion of Apprenticeship),
Reg Lang, Jack Ousley, Des Chatfield, Fred Denning, John Watts,
Mike Mullarky, Joe Hoyle, Jack Bauer, Gordon Smith, Ray Taylor,
Colin Heath, Brian Millward, Alan Millward (Boilersmith),
Glyn Protheroe, Percy Crabb, Ken Smith, Brian Joslin, Sam Hardy,
Ken Ware, Les Martin, Bill Palmer, George Palmer, David Luscombe, Andy Hosie, Pat Reid, Roy King, Bill Gates, Nat Clifford, Barry Quest, Robin Haterly, Ray Mallet, Bob Trevelyan.

Electricians taken on after Dieselization 1964-1967

David Clarke, 'Jock' Trotter, Percy Sellick, 'Pussy' Purrington

Boiler Inspector – Charlie Humphries, Vic Windsor.

Boilersmiths – Chargehand Jack Bonsfield, Ken Weare, Assist. Bill Eggerton, Brian 'Ginger' Joslin, Assist. Alfie Belcher, Joe Hawkins, Assist. Ernie 'CSM Horne.

Brick arch man – Michael Brooker.

Tuber and Stayer – Ron Morfet, Assist Ted Morbay.

Gland Packers – Bert 'Rosy' Rosevear, Harry 'Crabbie Passmore.

Overhead Crane drivers – Manny Coles, Walt White, Reg Fleming.

Staff transferred from Ashford after the works was bombed in 1940

Brindle Brown, Martin Lear, Bob Wilkinson, Charlie Smale, Jack Shillings, Percy Gibson, Joe Ditchberg (all Fitters), Bunny Oldstock (Coppersmith), 'Treacle' Keen (Blacksmith), 'Jumbo' James (Blacksmith Striker), Alfie Cook (Machinist), Alf Williams (Wheel Turner)

Other Grades
Lambert Gorwyn (Electrician for Bullied Pacific lighting)
Phil Issacs (Water Treatment)
Harry Passmore (Carpenter)

Shed Turners

These men were confined to the shed, usually due to medical reasons, their main duties being the correct placing of locos for their next duty or placing them in the shed for repairs; they would often be called upon to move or test an engine during or just after a repair.

Bill Godbear, Henry Turner, Fred Cole, Jack Hurrell, Jack Prendergast.

Office Staff

Horace Martin (Chief Clerk), Reg Purton, Gordan Tilley, John 'Flying Officer' , Fred (Pay Clerk), Charlie Hardwick (Time Clerk), Sammy Hanniford, Reg Brown (Time Clerk), Ron Sculpher (Time Clerk), Cecil Balment (Roster clerk), Douglas Simmons, Charlie Hurverd, David Blyth, David Bright.

Store Clerks

Fred King, Cecil Beaumont, John Ware, Ken Larcombe

Stores Issuers

Eric Cunningham, Michael Kennedy, Eddie Van Santen, Fred Partridge.

Secretary/Typist

Delma Salter (Daughter of Frank Salter)

Appendix 2

Footplate staff known to have worked at Exmouth Junction (1940 – 1967)

This list has been partially complied from the Engineman's Roster for 23 December 1955 and shows the pairing that then prevailed. Gaps indicate where men had not yet been allocated. The rest have been added as names were passed to the Author.

Driver
E Croft
Spreke
Parkhouse
Davison
Billen
Davey
Dack
Wollacott
F Turton
Smale
Wright
Isaac
R Cook
Horne
Harper
Gumm
M Spague
Barnes
R Radmore
J Baker
S P Burridge
Bolrill?
W Barriball
Jones
Nock
Beavis
A Crump
Carnell
Vinnicombe
F Churchill
H Yole
Huxham
E C Joslin
Biggs
E Barriball
R Dack
Bellworthy
G Spey
Heard
Hood
Brown
Cordery
Bradbury
Prigg
Bull
G Croft
F Burt
Pretty
Dinner
W Timms
Perkins
Spicer
R Jury
E Baker
Henley
H Westcott
L Grinney
Elliot
W Burridge
A Pope
Aplin
Crump
R Down

Fireman
Bartlett
G Phillips
Voaden
M Webb
Denman
Yeo
Wood
Munson
Trewin
Willey
Bewden
J Aplin
Nott
Parsons
Harland
Sene
Elsom
J Stephens
Cordial
Hearn
R Brown
Ridgeway
Clegg
R Burridge
Wilson
Seldon
R S Jones
G Hayman
Morrish
C Bond
Berry
Cudmore
Hawes
Shoulder
Daniels
P P Allen
Howard
G A Hooper
Sampson
Seward
G Smith
M Jones
Elston
Rockey
Rowsell
Tonkin
P Blake
England
Budd
Passmore
Bellamy
Hayfield
Hill
A C Brown
B Webber
Budd
T G Rowe
Emery
Wheeler
Betting
Fleming
Densham
Underhill

J Tucker
W Godbear
M Beavan

F Purrington
Milton
Padden

Law
Steer
Pridham
Passmore
Grant
Roberts
C Timms
F Turner
L Welling
Denning
C Melluish
T Cook
P Sprague
C Radmore

R Srague
Tanton
S Solman
J Stalves
M Pidgeon
Walker
E Snow
R Joslin
Hewitt
R A C Spague

Others listed, grades not known.

Special Leave
W Northem,
SV Burridge,

Sick
Mardon,
Hurrell,
G Westcott,
G Lodge,
L Dymond,
Hayman,
R Watts,
Carder.

Rest Days
Ley,
C Lodge,
W Lodge,
Luscombe,
Luxton,
Marchant,
A E Martin,
J A Martin,
JW Martin,
Medway,
Kelly,
Kennedy,
C King,

Dawe
E Beer
L Hayman
Williams
Baker
Johnson
R A Jones
B Dack
Spivey
P Solman
Cole
F Smith
Mudge
A R Turner
D Cook
Butler
Carnell
Bradford
Ballin
E Webb
Drew
Pym
F Bennellick
Russell

Oke
Potter
Cartwright
J Barriball
Rooke
D Chapman
P Bond

Lankster,
Larkworthy,
Lashbrook,
Lawrence,
LeMelliere,
Leverton,
Loman,
Mallet,
Mayne,
Morgam,
S A Jones,
W R Jones,
Kenshole,
I R D King,
Letten,
Lawrence,
Langman.

From Lyme Regis
Gage.

Foreman
H Turner.

Next Passed Man
Beer

Next Cleaner
Aggett

A not inconsiderable list and that was for just one day, two days before Christmas!

The following were footplate men at the shed 1947-1967, some took redundancy on closure others carried on their careers, in some cases moving away.

Frank Beasley
Bill Mudge
Reg Lancaster
Jim Cook
Harold Yeo
Jeff Sprague
"Be Be" Daniels
"Buster" Brown
Ken Belamy *(whose mother-in-law had been a cleaner during the war)*
E "Ted" or "Smokey" Crawforth
Ken "Jock" Pearson
Ray Hill
Mike Clements
Horace Stratford
Reg Pridham
Ernie Chowings
Les Stevens
Les Howard
Fred Butler (LDC)
Alfie Rowe
Graham Smith (Later Inspector)
Gordon Croft
Ken Croft
Eddie Goff
Richard Parkinson
Reg "Snowball" Richardson

Acknowledgements

A book of this style and nature would not have been possible without the help of the railwaymen who worked at Exmouth Junction. Special thanks go to Ted Crawforth, affectionately known as 'Smokey', for his help and enthusiasm. A tremendous amount of detailed information came from his diligently kept journals and records made during his time at The Junction, and these give a clear insight of the daily workings there. I would also like to thank the others in equal measure who gave their time and memories namely: G W Batten, E Goff, R Lang, B Russell, R Tacagni, R Taylor and the late F (John) Watts, plus those many others who heard of the project and gave details and additional names of those who worked there - their efforts form some of the Appendices at the back of the book.

For anyone seeking to under take a task such as this, a visit to the Newton Abbot Railway studies library is a must and I thank those there, both volunteers and the Librarian, for the information and help so freely given by them.

No book can succeed without photographs and this one is no exception, for this I owe a big debt of gratitude to Ted Crawforth for his faithful record of photos, also to Peter Gray, the late 'John' Watts, Reg Lang, Ray Taylor, Bill Batten, Bob Tacagni, Richard Holland, Amyas Crump, Bill Wright, the Rev. David Hardy, Maurice Dart and Eddie Goff.

Although not within the scope of this book, a special word of thanks is due for the tireless work of the the Rev. David Hardy who faithfully ministers to the railway family as a member of the Railway Mission and produces at no cost the thousands of photographs of the men who attend the annual retirement gathering at Exeter. To you all "Thank you".

Bibliography

'Growing Up on the Railway': Grace Horseman, Ark Publications 1998.

Articles on Exmouth Junction by "Smokey" Railway World magazine Feb/July 1981 and September 1982. Ian Allan

'British Railways Illustrated': Vol 7 7/04/98 "Corrugated to Concrete", Exmouth Junction 1878-1967 by Ian Sixsmith.

British Railway Magazines Southern Region: various.

Express and Echo Newspapers.

'Steam was my Calling': E S Beavor. Ian Allan 1974.

'Steam Motive Power Depots': E S Beavor. Ian Allan 1983.

'An Historical Survey of Southern Railway Sheds': Chris Hawkins & George Reeve 1979. Oxford Publishing Co.

'Rail Centres: Exeter': Colin Maggs. Ian Allan 1985.

'Devon's Railways': Mike Clements and Ted Gosling. Sutton Publishing.

'Bullied Last Giant of Steam': Sean Day-Lewis. George Allen & Unwin Ltd.